laugh!

Sam

THE SMART ALECK'S GUIDE TO THE BIBLE

vol. 1

SAM WRIGHT

SonRise Devotionals
Lighthouse Publishing of the Carolinas

THE SMART ALECK'S GUIDE TO THE BIBLE VOL. 1
BY SAM WRIGHT
SonRise Devotionals is an imprint of LPCBooks
a division of Iron Stream Media
100 Missionary Ridge, Birmingham, AL 35242

ISBN: 978-1-64526-278-7
Copyright © 2020 by Sam Wright
Cover design by Hannah Linder
Interior design by AtriTex Technologies P Ltd

Available in print from your local bookstore, online, or from the
publisher at: ShopLPC.com

For more information on this book and the author visit: author's
website URL here

Brought to you by the creative team at LPCBooks: Cindy
Sproles, Eva Marie Everson, and Jennifer Leo

Library of Congress Cataloging-in-Publication Data
Wright, Sam.
Smart Aleck's Guide to the Bible Vol. 1 / Sam Wright 1st ed.

Printed in the United States of America

Praises for
The Smart Aleck's Guide to the Bible

In "Smart Aleck's Guide to the Bible," one can laugh, cringe, be offended, or enjoy the creative, humor-based integration of modern cultural terms and social practices with actual scriptures straight from the Bible. The author "fills in the blanks," creates fantasies, and uses modern prospective to describe the Bible.

The Garden of Eden images are humorous and challenging since many of our modern social mores and prejudices are exposed as to their origin. The Noah and the Ark "between the lines" descriptions of life on the ark are humorous and realistic. Lawyer jokes and self-deprecating humor help the reader understand our patriarchal inclinations, and our tendency to procrastinate on biblical clarity about race, gender, sexuality, and most controversial issues. Dr. Wright has an "uncanny" insight into modern and biblical cultures and shows the ability to make you smile, cry, be mildly offended or befuddled. However, one never doubts the faith of the author and recognizes the sensitivity to controversy by the one who presents us these images and challenge us to think for our selves.

Dr. James Davis
President Emeritus, Shenandoah University,
and former Virginia legislator, RET.

The title might entice you to pick up this book, but Dr. Wrights subtlety, funny, and insightful one-liners open the Bible in a new way. You will laugh ... and you will think. Prepare to be entertained in new ways. Dr. Wright can turn a phrase, poke a little fun at himself, the reader ... and, yes, God. But all humor aside, this is a serious, readable biblical commentary for newcomers and longtime students. *Smart Aleck's Guide to the Bible* is a fresh look the Bible's opening. Biblical students will gain new insights, but this is also a great introduction for a skeptical, first time Bible reader. Dr. Wright would be a great dinner guest!

Frank H. Wheeler,
Chief Operating Officer of Baker and McKenzie, Ret.

Smart Aleck's Guide to the Bible sheds such a warm and humorous feel for the great stories in the Old Testament of the Bible. I laughed and even cried at some of the stories. I can envision readers using this book for devotions, sermon illustrations, or just for the fun of reading. Highly recommended!

Rev. Patty Daniels
Florida United Methodist Conference

Sam Wright is a serious thinker with a playful imagination. After fifty years in ministry, my wife and I have chosen him to be our pastor. Every week, we get ready to listen to his sermons knowing that first will come a humorous story. Laughing together gets us ready to listen together to his thoughtful reflection upon and application of the Word to our lives. I like Sam's angle of view in his reflections here. He asks questions, both playful and serious. He reminds us to stay in touch with our humanity. Stories we know by heart are opened up afresh by a loving heart, full of self-deprecation and honest confession. Sprinklings of theology mix with human foibles and lots of attitude. With a lighthearted touch, a lot of truth comes though. I wish my seminary professors had taught me the value of a sense of humor. This book is a fun read; I hope you will enjoy it too.

Dr. Kenneth L. Morrison
Pastor & Songwriter
When Christ Was Born of Mary Free What a Joy

Table of Contents

Introduction

*C*an the Holy Bible be a funny book? I believe so. There is, without doubt, humor in the Bible. Most of the time we miss it because we have been conditioned to be absolutely serious when reading the Bible.

Maybe we should blame the Puritans.

I believe that without some of our religious prejudices, we would probably chuckle from time to time as we read the text. We might even laugh out loud. In the strictest religious circles, if you smile when your Bible is lying open in front of you, you are guaranteed a ticket straight to hell. Without passing GO. Without collecting $200.

Before you get upset ... no, I am *not* writing to make fun of the Bible (although it may appear so to some Puritans). If you want to read a book that ridicules the Scriptures, then this book is not for you. In fact, I'm not suggesting we make fun of the Scriptures at all, but that we laugh when they make us laugh. In other words, we are not laughing *at* the text, but *with* the text.

When I read the Bible, I see God as a frustrated comedian, scratching His head and saying, "Why aren't people laughing? That's funny. I don't care who you are."

Where do you think Larry the Cable Guy got that line?

You may wonder what qualifies me to write this book. Well, I'll tell you: I am qualified to write this book because I am a smart aleck. And, I believe, God loves smart alecks. I actually think God laughs at some of Jim Carrey's movies—even *Bruce Almighty*, in which Carrey gets to be God (although it's easier for me to envision Morgan Freeman as God, or even George Burns).

As a certified smart aleck, I often see humor where others do not. However, I also understand that smart alecks can be very irritating to non-smart alecks. If you are easily annoyed by such people, you probably do not want to read this book. But I'm sure you have a smart-aleck friend who would love to read it and for whom you should purchase it.

I think smart alecks are God's favorites because we are not afraid to say what we think, even if we should not be thinking it. God is a God of grace (rather than lightning bolts)—which is especially important and good to know when you are a smart aleck.

When I was five years old, my mother tried to teach us about God's omnipresence. She said, "God is with us everywhere," to which I retorted, "Even in the bathroom?" It was in that moment that I learned God's judgment can be swift and unpleasant. I also realized that smart alecks are born and not made. No one had to teach me how to smart off.

It's been a lifelong gift.

Second, I am qualified to write about holy things because I am holy. Well, I'm supposed to be. I have served as an ordained pastor in the American Baptist Churches, USA, and then as an ordained elder in the United Methodist Church for decades. Ordination requires a certain level of sanctification. For example, if you end your prayer accidentally, "In the name of the Father, the Son, and the Holy Spigot," you cannot laugh, but must pretend that you said it correctly. If you are *really holy*, you will frown at those who snicker at your imagined mistake.

When I was a Baptist, I dared not acknowledge my parishioners in a liquor store. Now that I am Methodist, I can smile and dutifully mumble something about Holy Communion or note that Jesus turned the wash water into fine wine.

Third, I am a Bible nerd with a Ph.D. in biblical studies from The Southern Baptist Theological Seminary. You can't get any more serious about the Bible than that. I have had the privilege of teaching biblical studies in colleges and seminaries in the United States and in Brazil. And, despite my teaching, many of my students entered ordained ministry as priests, pastors, or ministers.

All that said, I hope smart alecks like me or smart-alecks-in-training will enjoy my moments of hilarity with the Word of God. Let's start where it all began: *in the beginning.*

1
Was God Afraid of the Dark?

In the beginning when God created the heavens and the earth, the earth was a formless void and darkness covered the face of the deep, while a wind from God swept over the face of the waters. Then God said, "Let there be light"; and there was light. And God saw that the light was good; and God separated the light from the darkness. God called the light Day, and the darkness he called Night. And there was evening and there was morning, the first day.

Genesis 1:1-5

By asking this question I tempt the Almighty to strike me with a lightning bolt. But think about what happens in the first few verses of Genesis. God says, "Let there be light" and it happens. God sees the light is good. If this is true, then presumably the darkness is bad. Is God afraid of the dark? No "nightlight" in the universe so God created light? How long has God been in the dark?

I don't want to ask, "How long did it take God to turn on the light?" It is not a lightbulb joke. But it makes you wonder.

Surely God can see in the dark, or else my mother never would have told me that God could see me all the time, and knew everything I was doing.

God thinks light is good. I agree. If you've ever tried to find the bathroom in the dark of a hotel room so as not to wake your wife, you know that light is good and darkness is bad. You may have a broken toe to prove it.

God brings order to the chaos and created light by speaking. I envy God in this. As the man of the house, I sometimes tried to bring order out of chaos. I tried God's approach. I would say with all the authority I could muster, "This is how it's going to be!" But instead of light breaking into existence or plants springing from the earth, all I got were smirks and eye-rolls. I was relieved later to find God experiences this, too.

God creates the heavens and the earth. God and God alone is the subject of this verb "create" (bara') in the Hebrew Bible. This action of creation is something that only God can do. God creates by speaking. When God speaks, things happen.

Pastors enjoy that power as well. We say to the congregation, "Please stand." In high church it's "Let us rise." In low church, "Git to your feet." When the pastor says these words, amazingly everyone gets to their feet, except for the few in wheelchairs. And in certain denominations, they are encouraged to stand as well.

Choir directors have even more power. They don't even speak. They just raise their hands, palms up, and the entire choir stands ... except for the tenor who was checking his phone for messages at that moment.

God creates the world and invents light to shine in all our darkness. I don't know about you, but I need all the light I can get, especially when I ask such questions and I hope to say of God with the psalmist: *It is you who light my lamp; the Lord, my God, lights up my darkness* (Psalm 18:28).

2
Is God Married?

Then God said, "Let us make humankind in our image,
according to our likeness; and let them have dominion
over the fish of the sea, and over the birds of the air, and
over the cattle, and over all the wild animals of the earth,
and over every creeping thing that creeps upon the earth."
So God created humankind in his image,
in the image of God he created them;
male and female he created them.

Genesis 1:26-27

ho is with God? Is God married? Is there a Mrs. God?

In the Ancient Near East, we would expect God to have a consort, a female counterpart. But the Bible has few hints of such theology. In fact, this fact makes the Hebrew Scriptures distinct from other ancient Near

Eastern religious texts. God is one. There is no God-couple as one may find in ancient pantheons. There is no Mrs. God.

What does it mean to be created in the image of God? This story has male and female created at the same time. Apparently, the image of God can only be reflected in both genders—male and female. At the most basic level to create people "in our image, according to our likeness" means that people look like God. These same words, "likeness" and "image" are used in Genesis 5:3 to describe Seth, who was the "spitting image" of his dad. (This makes one wonder about Cain and Abel, who are not described that way.)

So, we look like God? Does it mean God walks upright, with two arms and two legs?

Are we made in the image of God in the way a street artist might draw a person's caricature? Does the male image of God look like Mr. Universe and the female image look like Miss Universe? Are even these physical specimens more like cartoon characters of God?

Lately God's image seems to be getting more and more paunchy—at least in America. Psalm 2:4 says, "God sits in the heavens and laughs." Is God saying, "Really? No way. I don't look like that. That person makes me look fat." Then God laughs with a big belly laugh—sorry, Lord—with a taut six-pack chuckle.

For most of us, the answer to what it means to be created in the image of God has to be deeper than that.

In the context of Chapter One, could it be that God has dominion, and to be created in the image of God is to have dominion? Or does it mean that we were made to live ethically and morally, like the holy Creator?

No matter how we think of it, from God's perspective, with the way we humans act, especially in these days, we must be like the Cartoon Network to God.

Yet despite the bad that people do, or the good we fail to do, God created us to be *like God*. God put us in charge, which may make us question God's judgment.

The Lord apparently believes in us more than we do.

3
We Got One Right

God blessed them, and God said to them, "Be fruitful
and multiply, and fill the earth and subdue it; and have
dominion over the fish of the sea and over the birds of the
air and over every living thing that moves upon the earth."

Genesis 1:28

According to some counts there are 613 commands in the Pentateuch[i]. From all perspectives, humans' track record on keeping these commands is not good. We might even imagine that humanity has received an "F" on its report card.

Some might argue that it's not all that bad. How many of us have ever boiled a baby goat in its mother's milk as described in Exodus 23:19? *The choicest of the*

---

i   The Pentateuch is the first five books of the Old Testament.

first fruits of your ground you shall bring into the house of the LORD your God, it reads. *You shall not boil a kid in its mother's milk.*

Maybe we've kept a few more just because most of us don't raise goats or have bulls that might gore someone. Perhaps we have not broken all the commands, but it's not for a lack of trying.

We violate biblical laws by doing such things as wearing cotton and polyester blends, which is against Leviticus 19:19, coveting our neighbor's Porsche (sort of mentioned in Exodus 20:17), eating a rare steak (Leviticus 19:26), not rising before an elderly person (Leviticus 19:32), not loving our neighbor (Leviticus 19:18), or working on Saturday, which is *Shabbat,* or the Sabbath (Exodus 20:10).

However (drumroll, please) we have *excelled* at keeping one law in particular. We are super at being fruitful. Don't believe it? Run to your computer, put your cursor into the oblong box of your favorite search engine, and ask how many people live on this planet. Go ahead. I'll wait … That's right! More than seven *billion*!

I have a suggestion for God. If all the other rules were as enjoyable to keep as what leads to being fruitful, perhaps we would have gotten an A on more of them. Just sayin'.

4

Grading Your Own Paper

God said, "See, I have given you every plant yielding
seed that is upon the face of all the earth, and every tree
with seed in its fruit; you shall have them for food. And to
every beast of the earth, and to every bird of the air, and
to everything that creeps on the earth, everything that has
the breath of life, I have given every green plant for food."
And it was so. God saw everything that he had made,
and indeed, it was very good. And there was evening and
there was morning, the sixth day.

Genesis 1:29-31

At this point it looks like God's intent is for all creatures to be vegetarian. Did plants get a vote in this? Did the carnivores have a say? Is God a vegetarian? A vegan, perhaps? We will address *that* issue in a later chapter, but for now let's see how God evaluates the six-day project of creating the world.

Remember back in school when you had to grade your own paper? After the spelling quiz the teacher would say, "Now you are going to grade your papers. Everyone grade your own work. I will say the correct spelling. Mark an X beside each one you get wrong. Then pass your papers forward."

I won the spelling bee in our class in 6th grade. You might think that was a good thing, but it created problems for me. The pressure was tremendous. One day I misspelled one of the 20 words on the weekly spelling test. What if one of the other kids noticed and brought it to the attention of the whole class? How would that affect my champion status? We were grading our own papers, so I erased the wrong spelling to write in the correct word rather than marking an X by it.

But I could not go through with it. Why? No, not because my conscience sidled up next to me. My eraser kept me honest. It didn't do a good enough job of erasing. It would have been obvious that I cheated. So I had to trace back over the mostly erased wrongly spelled word and place an X by it.

Can you imagine the pressure on God at the time of creation? God is evaluated on everything in the world all the time. In this passage God thinks the work of creating the universe is stellar. "God saw everything that he had made, and indeed, it was very good."

Now this raises some important theological questions. Is "very good" an A+, an A or an A-, or perhaps even (don't strike me, Lord!) a B+? It depends on whether you think there could be a better way to design a platypus or a giraffe. Should horseflies and mosquitos be considered errors? A pitcher who takes a line drive in the groin might argue that certain male parts should have been created on the inside. Female mammals might argue that live births are hard on everyone. The husband passed out on the delivery room floor would probably also agree. So, why not come up with a better process of bringing little ones into the world? Maybe Amazon has the right idea with drone deliveries.

It also might make a difference what criteria we use. If you are judge at a Miss Universe Pageant, you have a different set of specimens than if you are weighing in newcomers at Weight Watchers.

I remember a little kid who asked why God lets people die and keeps having to make new ones. He wanted to know why God doesn't just keep the ones he has. I think his question came after the arrival of a baby sister.

Ah, the whole growing-old-and-dying process. What's up with that? Why does one's eyesight begin to decline after age eleven and overall health after age twenty-seven? Why couldn't we just keep getting better with age, like fine wine? Imagine if the best athletes were in their 70s, 80s, and 90s.

The more thought we give to this, the more we might not agree with such high marks for God's handiwork. But then, maybe we have to stick to grading our own papers.

5
God Takes a Personal Day

Thus the heavens and the earth were finished, and all their multitude. And on the seventh day God finished the work that he had done, and he rested on the seventh day from all the work that he had done. So God blessed the seventh day and hallowed it, because on it God rested from all the work that he had done in creation.

Genesis 2:1-4

What is the climax of this creation story? Wouldn't it be the creation of humans, male and female, in the image of God? You would think so. The story clearly pinnacles at this point. God blesses several parts of creation, including humans. However, God declares only one thing holy—the Sabbath.

We might disagree with God on this. We would

suggest that the human form is sacred, at least some versions of us. Hasn't God seen Michelangelo's *David* or certain firefighter calendars? How could God ignore the Miss Universe contest? Many of us want to look like these divine specimens through gym memberships, weight loss plans, and plastic surgery. But God only makes the seventh day holy.

People often have asked me if God created the world in six 24-hour days. First, that is the way the writer intends for us to understand it because the climax is God's hallowing the seventh day and taking the day off. Apparently, even God lives for the weekend.

Second, we should not take this story literally to try to argue against any scientific theories about evolution or the big-bang theory. The Bible is not a book of science, but a book about God. Religion and science are two different ways of approaching the world, even if they aren't at odds with each other. It's sort of like how my wife's approach to movies is different from mine. To her a good movie is when you cry so hard you get your popcorn soggy. I prefer action and adventure … a heroic last man standing who has saved the day. (And, yes, it's okay if he has the girl standing with him at the end.)

The church "borrowed" the idea of resting on the Sabbath—Saturday—and applied it to Sunday. When I was growing up, my mother insisted on us taking naps on Sunday afternoon. I hated taking naps. We had to lay on our beds. We were forbidden to talk or read. We were supposed to be resting. I could not sleep. I was bored out of my mind. I'm sure that is not what God intended for Sunday afternoons. To make matters worse, we were in church for two hours on Sunday morning then three hours every Sunday evening. Talk about a wasted day, at least from a kid's perspective. And to add insult to injury, because we went to the Sunday evening service, we missed *The Wonderful World of Disney*.

I could certainly have rested better in front of the TV. My wife says I've made up for it since then.

God rested. Does God need to rest? Well, God *is* older than you think. He is called "The Ancient of Days" in Daniel. I think Daniel is being quite considerate. He could have called God the "Ancient of Millennia." Not to be rude, but think how tired you'd be if you had been around for eternity. Even saying, "Let there be . . ." might take a lot out of you if you've been around that long.

And what's up with starting the day in the evening at sundown? So you go to sleep a few hours after a new day starts. Is God taking this idea of resting a little too far? People used to say, "It's a man's world." But is it really—and I ask this with all due respect—the Old Man's world?

I said, "WITH ALL DUE RESPECT, O ANCIENT OF DAYS, IT'S YOUR WORLD."

6

Wanted: Gardener to Care for Small Patch of Paradise

In the day that the Lord God made the earth and the heavens, when no plant of the field was yet in the earth and no herb of the field had yet sprung up—for the Lord God had not caused it to rain upon the earth, and there was no one to till the ground; but a stream would rise from the earth, and water the whole face of the ground— then the Lord God formed man from the dust of the ground, and breathed into his nostrils the breath of life; and the man became a living being. And the Lord God

planted a garden in Eden, in the east; and there he put the
man whom he had formed.

Genesis 2:4b-8

*G*od creates a man because God needs a gardener. Apparently, no one responded to God's ad for a gardener in the classifieds or on Craigslist. So God makes a man ('adam in Hebrew) from the ground ('adamah in Hebrew) to be the gardener.

In this second story, God does not *speak* humans into existence. Instead God gets his hands dirty. God fashions a man from the dirt, like a child might form something out of Play-Doh … except God is *really* good at it. Then God breathes into man's nostrils the "breath of life." Not only is God willing to get his hands dirty in making man from dirt, he gets his mouth dirty as well.

Someone needs to give God a class in CPR. That's not how you do it! Not the nostrils—the mouth. Is this the origin of sinus problems in humans? Is this why we say, "God bless you" when someone sneezes? What does it mean, theologically speaking, when someone has allergies?

God creates the man to work for Him. The man is basically "breathed-on dirt." God's breath makes the human alive. What shall we call this God-breathing into the human? Holytosis?

After getting His hands dirty making the man, God plants a garden. God is into horticulture. God loves playing in the dirt. But this God wants the help of a human to keep His garden going.

Are farmers closer to God because they work in the dirt, like God did? Is agribusiness God's business? I've known farmers who would claim this is true. God provides all kinds of fruit for the human to eat. Even though the man has to work, there is the impression that things grow easily in God's garden. This is Eden, after all.

Food was scarce and always required a great deal of work for most people throughout the history of the ancient Near East. In paradise, fruit trees produce in abundance. The man's food is plentiful, fresh, and healthy. No cheese fries, rocky road ice cream, deep-dish pizza, or chocolate. How could this possibly be called *paradise*?

All the trees are beautiful. "Out of the ground the LORD God made to grow every tree that is pleasant to the sight and good for food." No thorn trees. No sour lemon trees. No ugly fruit trees.

Two trees are mentioned specifically—"the tree of life also in the midst of the garden, and the tree of the knowledge of good and evil." These will become important in the next scene.

For much of humanity, enjoying plentiful food would be paradise. To live among beautiful trees in conversation with God would be beyond what we can imagine. In this ancient story, humanity is created to serve God as gardeners. Both creation stories suggest that humans are responsible to God for the earth.

Kinda makes you wonder why we haven't been fired.

7
The First Diet

The Lord God took the man and put him in the garden of Eden to till it and keep it. And the Lord God commanded the man, "You may freely eat of every tree of the garden; but of the tree of the knowledge of good and evil you shall not eat, for in the day that you eat of it you shall die."

Genesis 2:15-17

We only hear God's side of the conversation in these verses. But I imagine it went like this:

God says, "You may eat of every tree of the garden."

Adam says, "That's great. There are so many, and the trees are so full of fruit. I can't wait to try them all. I am intrigued by this round one with the red skin. What's this one called?" Adam reaches out his hand to pick the fruit.

God steps between Adam and the tree and says, "But of this tree of the knowledge of good and evil, you shall not eat."

Adam whines, "But it looks *so good*. Can't I just have one bite? Why can't I have it? You said I could eat from every tree in the garden." (Insert foot stomping here.)

God clarifies, "From all of them except this one."

"What's the problem? You created it, so it has to be good, right?"

God warns, "On the day you eat from it, you shall surely die."

Like most children, man continues in his argument. "Why? If it's a tree for knowing, wouldn't that be a good thing? I have not had much of an education. You know a mind is a terrible thing to waste. Besides if I have to *take care* of that tree, why can't I taste its fruit? Doesn't seem fair to me."

God just shakes his head and points to the abundance of other fruit trees.

Is this like dangling a carrot in front of a donkey? "Look, you can have all these, but *this one* you cannot have." What do we do? What are we interested in? The one that is forbidden. Isn't this every human's nature? Once the line is drawn, some people will step over it immediately. Others will try to put it out of their minds without success. Then they will wonder what that fruit tastes like, what it feels like, and so on until sooner or later, we all come around to the forbidden tree. The story of the Garden of Eden is *our* story, the human story.

I love sweets. I am most successful losing weight when I quit eating sweets altogether. We remove all sweets from our house. That makes it much easier to avoid the temptation. But bring one bar of chocolate into the house ...

By putting the tree of knowledge of good and evil in the middle of the garden, God sets up the man (and woman). Of course, it's also a test because there is always temptation to disobey, to go astray. Even though we do not keep sweets in the house, there will be the church dinner with all those delicious pies, cakes, and cookies calling my name.

So maybe it's not so much a set-up for the story, but a description of life and how we give in to temptation.

But I'm getting ahead of the story ...

8
Trying to Make Partner

Then the LORD God said, "It is not good that the man
should be alone; I will make him a helper as his partner."
So out of the ground the LORD God formed every animal
of the field and every bird of the air, and brought them to
the man to see what he would call them; and whatever the
man called every living creature, that was its name. The
man gave names to all cattle, and to the birds of the air,
and to every animal of the field; but for the man there was
not found a helper as his partner.

Genesis 2:18-20

God realizes that the man needs a partner, someone to help him with his work. Why? Because he's not keeping up with the work? Or because he is lonely? Perhaps when God made Adam, he whistled while he worked. But there is no Snow White here to make him laugh or to help him. And he knows to stay away from the one poison apple tree among the myriad of trees.

Apparently, God gets his hands dirty again, fashioning creatures of all kinds from the mud and breathing life into them. I don't want to picture that myself. Is God putting his mouth to the nostrils of each? It's like God is blowing up balloon animals, animating them and handing them off to Adam. Adam gets to name them. But it's more than a naming process. They are looking for a "helper as a partner for the man."

God and Adam are not successful. "But for the man there was not found a helper as his partner" has to be one of the funniest lines in the Bible. In this passage God is like Thomas Edison, who experimented with thousands of substances before he discovered tungsten for his light bulb. Can you imagine Adam telling this story to Eve? She responds, "You and God did *that?*" Then she rolls on the ground laughing.

"Making partner" has a whole new meaning. I can picture God bringing his creations to Adam and pointing out their positive attributes.

"What about the yellow Labrador? She's friendly. She'll be loyal to you forever."

"Yeah. But she's always sticking her cold nose in my warm places when I'm not expecting it. And when she gets wet, she stinks to high heaven. Couldn't I have someone with only two legs?"

"What about the orangutan? Smart as you are."

"Yeah, but she's always two steps ahead of me in checkers."

"The chimp? Lots of fun."

"She's never serious."

"What do you have to be serious about?" God asks.

"Besides, she steals my bananas," Adam adds.

The naming process would not be simple. The zebra complains, "Why do I have to be at the end of the alphabet? Why does the aardvark get to be the first one on the list?"

"He has a nose for it," Adam says, then laughs at his own joke.

The polar bear asks, "What if I move to the Bronx? What's polar about that?"

"That's cool, like Indiana Jones, who was not from Indiana," says Adam.

Complaints from the hyena, the platypus, and the emu follow.

The loudest complaint comes from the "dung beetle."

"But that's what you do," Adam retorts, "You roll dung balls."

Adam is exhausted from his naming all the animals, when the competitions begin.

The sea creatures, who have been shut out of the competitions, protest. The dolphin is the main spokesperson. She argues that she could be the best partner because she is a fast swimmer, intelligent, and has a great laugh. And she will never let him drown. After swimming with the dolphin, Adam acknowledges that she would make a good partner, but he takes off points because he cannot keep up with her and she is smarter than he is. God says, "Adam, you probably should not rule anyone out on that basis. No doubt, your partner also will probably need a good sense of humor."

In the end, Adam eliminates the sea creatures because the saltwater dries his skin.

The competition for the strongest provides interesting drama. Adam has come up with the five finalists: the tiger, the grizzly, the elephant, the ox, and the gorilla. But before the final round, a formal protest is lodged by the insect world. They threaten a class-action discrimination lawsuit against the human and God. However, they cannot find an attorney.

And this is paradise.

The reptile world also requests a meeting with Adam. Only the anaconda shows up. They never find out what happened to the others. She belches and says, "Look I represent all the constrictors. I can squeeze to death anything that tries to bother you, up to my own weight."

"How much do you weigh?" asks Adam.

"You don't need to know that. Just know that no one can hug you like I can. You will never forget it when I hug you."

Adam shivers and bids the snake adieu. She hisses, "You'll be sorry for snubbing us snakes," as she slithers away. "I have brothers ..."

At that moment the eagle lands on Adam's shoulder. She digs her claws in just a tiny bit. "You know I'm the strongest of all birds. I can lift and carry something four times my own body weight." "Wow!" says Adam, "That would be great for deliveries. You could fetch me fish every day."

"Adam, you still are a vegetarian, remember."

"Oh, that's right."

"Stay with the script."

Adam apologizes to the sea creatures, the reptiles and the birds. He says, "Sorry, but for this strongest-creature competition, I'm sticking with the mammals." He finally pronounces the winner of the strongest creature competition is the elephant. An argument explodes.

The tiger yells, "Look I can carry something twice my own weight up a tree. You've got to consider agility too."

The grizzly counters, "But you carry it with your teeth. Yuck!"

The ox just moans until Adam says, "I may use you later."

The gorilla is furious. He has been posing all this time in his best Mr. Universe stance. He picks up a

4,000-pound boulder and throws it at the elephant. The elephant in turn catches it and tosses it back at the gorilla. Dodge boulder.

Then comes the beauty pageant.

The chameleon steps up first. "Look," she says, as she changes from green to purple. "I can be whatever color you want, Adam. I can match whatever outfit you are wearing."

Adam looks down and says, "Wearing?"

God says, "You may need help in this department."

The blue and yellow macaw lands on a branch in front of Adam. "Very impressive," Adam says. Then he is distracted as an iridescent Blue Morpho butterfly flits by whispering his name.

The zebra trots by. "Stripes are in, you know."

The tiger says, "You want stripes. Look here."

Then the giraffe steps up and says, "But my print is fabulous."

"I've got patterns to die for," the leopard chimes.

"But I'm prettier," the jaguar proclaims.

"Simple dots are more elegant," the cheetah declares.

"I'm with her," the Dalmatian demands. "Besides, black and white are in."

The panda whispers, "You like black and white? How about me."

The black panther states that "Black is beautiful."

The polar bear roars, "So is white!"

The bald eagle swoops in just to show off.

The peacock struts his stuff, displaying his plumage.

The hummingbird flashes her colors by hovering around Adam's head.

And then Adam, poor tired Adam, sighs. "This is too complicated," he says with a yawn. "I think I need a nap."

9
She Is Built!

So the LORD God caused a deep sleep to fall upon the
man, and he slept; then he took one of his ribs and closed
up its place with flesh. And the rib that the LORD God
had taken from the man he made (built) into a woman
and brought her to the man. Then the man said,
"This at last is bone of my bones
and flesh of my flesh;
this one shall be called Woman,
for out of Man this one was taken."

Genesis 2:21-23

Adam slumps in the grass, exhausted. God is not too happy with the way things have gone because they have not been able to find a helper for Adam.

God finally decides to try another approach. "What would make you happy, Adam?"

Adam says, "I want someone more like me … but with curves."

God asks, "What do you mean by curves?"

"I'm not exactly sure. You're the creative one."

"What else do you want?"

"I want someone who will cook all my food, have sex with me whenever I want, and do whatever I tell her."

"That is going to cost you."

"How much?"

"An arm and a leg," says God.

Adam pauses for a moment to think then asks, "What can I get for a rib?"[ii]

God performs the first surgery and creates a woman to be the man's helper.

What does the word "helper" mean? The word helper ('ezer) is not a demeaning term. It does not refer to a servant or a slave. God is not making an employee—an assistant gardener—for the man to supervise. Rather God is making a partner—someone to work alongside the man, someone to be his companion. In fact, the verb "to help" in Hebrew is often used of God helping Israel.

When I was an adolescent and we talked about a young woman being "built," who knew we were biblically correct? The Hebrew word for "made" in this

---

ii   Author is unsure as to the origin of this joke, but has
          heard it from pulpits as long as he can remember.

verse is not the normal verb for "to make" but means most often "build," as in building a house.

God's building project clearly excites Adam. It's love at first sight. And you know a man is in love when he starts writing poetry. Adam says,

> "This at last is bone of my bones
>   and flesh of my flesh;
>   this one shall be called Woman,
>   for out of Man this one was taken."

I love the old adage, "Woman was not taken out of man's head to rule over him. Nor was she taken out of man's feet to serve him. She was taken out of man's side to come alongside him and be his companion."

Of course, there is another "ancient" version of this story.

Even though the garden was beautiful and the fruit delicious, Eve complains to God that she is lonely and bored.

God says, "I'll take care of that. I'll make a man for you."

Eve asks, "What's a man?"

God says, "A man is a wonderful creature who will be bigger and stronger than you. He will want to protect you and provide for you. He will kill things and bring them home for you to cook. He will try to satisfy your physical needs. He will be irritating in some ways. He will not be as good at communicating as you are.

Listening will be a challenge for him, especially if there is a ballgame on. He will not be as intelligent as you are."

Eve: "That doesn't sound too bad. Is there anything else I should know?"

God: "Yes. He will have a big ego. So even though he will need your advice, you'll have to make him think it was his idea. Also, you will have to let him think I created him first."[iii]

Even though God involves the man in the creation by naming the animals, God is clearly the superior being. It may be that the experiment of forming the animals to find a partner is not so much for God to see what works but for the man to appreciate his wife when she finally is created. Think about it, Adam, *you almost married the orangutan.*

God is the first anesthetist and the first surgeon. Medical costs have been going up ever since.

Adam's excitement at Eve's creation reminds us of the hope that springs eternal in the human heart, when love is fresh and strong and young (or deaf, blind, and stupid). This is where we want to read the fairy-tale ending, "And they lived happily ever after." However, that's not the ending of the biblical story, because Adam and Eve's story is our story.

The Bible says, "Therefore a man leaves his father and his mother and clings to his wife, and they become one

---

iii   Source unknown.

flesh. And the man and his wife were both naked, and were not ashamed." Of course, they had not discovered the forbidden fruit and gained 25 pounds either.

We really want to know what all the kids in high school want to know—are they having sex?

Does being naked and "becoming one flesh" mean they were having sex? Our answer to that question reveals how we view human bodies in general. Those who understand human bodies as good and sex created by God for humans to enjoy may assume that naturally they were having sexual relations. Picture Woodstock.

Those who have a darker view of the material world may assume that they weren't having sex until they ate from the tree of the knowledge of good and evil or that the eating of the forbidden pomegranate is really a metaphor for the sexual act and the subsequent loss of innocence. Picture a nun smacking your knuckles for drawing an anatomically correct Adam and Eve in your notebook.

Even in the Bible there are different ideas about God and about how we fit into God's universe. The first story promotes humanity as created in the image of God. Humans are blessed. The male and female images of God are told to be fruitful and multiply in the world where everything is pronounced good. Sex is good. Babies are good. The second story portrays man as breathed-on dirt. Then Eve was made from Adam's rib.

So, was God saying, "I can do better"?

10
The Snake Was Right

Now the serpent was more crafty than any other wild
animal that the LORD God had made. He said to the
woman, "Did God say, 'You shall not eat from any tree in
the garden'?" The woman said to the serpent, "We may eat
of the fruit of the trees in the garden; but God said, 'You
shall not eat of the fruit of the tree that is in the middle
of the garden, nor shall you touch it, or you shall die.'" But
the serpent said to the woman, "You will not die; for God
knows that when you eat of it your eyes will be opened,
and you will be like God, knowing good and evil." So
when the woman saw that the tree was good for food, and
that it was a delight to the eyes, and that the tree was to
be desired to make one wise, she took of its fruit and ate;
and she also gave some to her husband, who was with her,
and he ate. Then the eyes of both were opened, and they

knew that they were naked; and they sewed fig leaves
together and made loincloths for themselves.

Genesis 3:1-7

First, we need to address the snake, or at least acknowledge that he could be addressed, and respond. We find talking animals in fables, but in the Bible? I mean, *a talking snake?*

Two times animals speak in the Bible—the snake here and Balaam's donkey in Numbers 22. The donkey had to be beaten three times before she said a word. The snake, on the other hand, seems eager to converse.

Since this is part of the creation story, perhaps we should assume all the animals could communicate with humans. Is this an ability that humans lost when we got kicked out of the garden? Were the animals so disappointed with our species, they made an eternal pact never to converse with humans again with the exception of a few YouTube dogs?

The snake has read the rental agreement. No, I'm not suggesting the serpent was an attorney. Not another lawyer joke—at least, not yet. But he is, the Bible tells us, *crafty*.

There is a play on the word *crafty* with the word *naked* in the previous verse—*and the man and his wife were both naked, and were not ashamed* (2:25) in that they are the same word in Hebrew ('arum). The couple is naked ('arum). The snake is wise/crafty ('arum). The man and woman will become wise or crafty ('arum) when they eat from the tree of knowing good and evil and realize they are naked ('arum).

This puts a whole new light on the church ladies' *craft* fair.

The snake knows God will not kill the man and woman if they eat the forbidden fruit. The serpent says they will not die and they will be like God, knowing good and evil. Is anything that the snake says untrue? No. The snake is absolutely correct. They do not die, *plus* they suddenly have knowledge they did not have before, becoming more like God.

And I wonder … at this point, did their conversation suddenly change?

"Hey, Eve, I like your outfit, but you're naked. Get some clothes on! What are you doing streaking through the garden?"

"Honey, would you cover that thing up? It's distracting."

Here's where Eve gets a bad rap. Eve was not there when God spoke to Adam about not eating from this particular tree. Some theologians and other Bible readers have made a big deal out of the fact that Eve adds that they are not to touch the fruit to the original commandment—thus changing the word of God. My mother taught me that if you touch a cookie, then see a bigger cookie on the plate, you have to take the one you touched—not the bigger one. Perhaps as the mother of all mothers, Eve knows that if you touch it, you have to eat it.

Those who blame Eve imply that Adam is less to blame. But what does the text actually say? Where is Adam when Eve eats the pomegranate? (You thought it was an apple, didn't you?) Eve eats from the pomegranate, then, "she also gave some to her husband, who was with her, and he ate."

How do we interpret the phrase "her husband, who was with her"? Is Adam "with her" in the sense that Adam is watching a ballgame while the serpent is having this conversation with his wife in the kitchen? How is he to notice she put a bowl of forbidden pomegranate down next to the chips and dip?

Is Adam "with her" in the sense that he is at home but tinkering in the backyard? He is trying to create his own crew of gardeners by forming little human clay figures from the mud and blowing on them.

If Eve is *deceived*, is Adam just plain *stupid*? Or, should we give him more credit and assume he is "with her" in the sense that he is paying attention to the snake's assertion and agreeing with what Eve concludes—that they should eat the fruit?

Later, male writers will blame Eve for being deceived. Eve is intelligent and curious. She is paying attention to the snake and investigating the fruit. Clearly, she is the smarter kid in this class.

There is an ancient tradition from the Gnostics that Eve was a hero for pursuing knowledge. Gnostics believed that finding special knowledge would lead to salvation. So, they lifted Eve up as the first who was curious and sought out knowledge. She became their patron saint.

Eve is tempted because the forbidden fruit looks better, tastes better, and makes you smarter than all the other fruit. Is this fair? It's like putting plates of celery, broccoli, bean sprouts, radishes and wilted lettuce around the table and a platter of warm chocolate chip cookies in the middle. As the aroma of the freshly baked cookies fills their nostrils, you tell your kids, "Kids, enjoy the vegetables, but don't eat the cookies."

Right. Like that's going to happen.

But maybe that's the point of the story—we always give in to temptation.

I believe it was Mae West who said, "I can resist anything but temptation."

Even though everything the snake says is true, the snake does not tell the whole story. And isn't that the problem with temptation? We look only at the good side, the appealing side. We refuse to consider all the consequences of our giving in to temptation. Or we minimize and deny them. Of course, we cannot always foresee the fallout from succumbing to our impulses. Adam and Eve are *not* expecting an eviction notice.

The negative outcomes are in the fine print, which no one reads. The dessert will be delicious. The fine print—you will gain five pounds. Ten miles over the speed limit will get me to work on time. The fine print—speeding fines doubled in a construction zone. Okay … I know … it's large print on road signs, but we can still ignore it. We don't think about the consequences. We pretend we can avoid them.

But back to our story: After eating a bite of fruit, Adam and Eve are enlightened. "Hey, we're naked!"

Are we talking about sex here? Some scholars think so. And it would make sense. Should we understand this passage figuratively? Could be. But the Bible is usually up front saying when people have sex—the Hebrew expression is "he knew her," which means sexual intercourse. And the "knowing" usually results in: "and she conceived and bore a son."

So, there are consequences to our actions. God had said that the day they ate of the forbidden fruit, they would die. God gave permission for the man to eat from any fruit—*but of the tree of the knowledge of good and evil you shall not eat, for in the day that you eat of it you shall die* (Genesis 2:17). The Hebrew is emphatic, literally: "dying you shall die."

Was God promising to execute the man if he disobeyed or warning that the fruit was poisonous? Or had God "over-threatened" like many parents do? "If you skip school again, it will be the last time you ever skip anything. Remember I brought you into this world and I can take you out."

God is wrong; the snake is right. The man and woman do not die. At least not on the spot. Is it God's compassion and grace? Or does God not want to scrap the whole human creation experiment and start all over—at least not yet?

Thank God, we don't get everything we deserve.

11
New Games with God

They heard the sound of the Lord God walking in the garden at the time of the evening breeze, and the man and his wife hid themselves from the presence of the Lord God among the trees of the garden. But the Lord God called to the man, and said to him, "Where are you?" He said, "I heard the sound of you in the garden, and I was afraid, because I was naked; and I hid myself."

Genesis 3:8-10

*H*ide and Seek.

Many years ago, my wife, our son, and I were in Amman, Jordan, for four days in the month of September. In the evening, as the heat of the day was abruptly and partially alleviated by a strong breeze that kicked up then, people poured out of their homes to take a walk.

Apparently, something similar happened in the evening in the Garden of Eden—this was the time God took His walks.

After the man and woman realize they are naked, they hide themselves. But, like three-year-old children, they are not very good at it. Have you ever played "Hide and Seek" with a preschooler? You can tell them to go hide, and they will. Then you count and say, "Ready or not, here I come." If you ask, "Where are you?" They will say, "Here I am." They understand the hiding part, but haven't quite caught on to the "not-being-found" aspect of the game. Like them, when God asks where Adam is, the first man steps out from the bushes just like a preschooler, and starts talking.

I heard the sound of you in the garden, and I was afraid, because I was naked; and I hid myself.

Does God make noise when he walks? Does He have squeaky shoes? Have you ever walked in front of a crowded room, and every step announced your coming? What size shoe does God wear? I remember as a kid having new jeans (back before they "distressed" jeans). Every step you took the jeans would rub together making a loud enough noise that all the kids in the class would look up to see what kind of broom the janitor was using. Corduroys were worse. Maybe God had gotten new jeans or new shoes.

Either way, Adam begins the "Passing the Buck" game. *He* [God] *said, "Who told you that you were naked?*

Have you eaten from the tree of which I commanded you not to eat?" The man said, "The woman whom you gave to be with me, she gave me fruit from the tree, and I ate." Then the Lord God said to the woman, "What is this that you have done?" The woman said, "The serpent tricked me, and I ate" (Genesis 3:11-13).

If it is true that we all give in to temptation, it is equally true that we blame others for our own failures. When God confronts Adam with his disobedience, Adam defends himself—*the woman you gave me,* he says. A great line spoken with a lot of moxie. He blames both God and the woman in one phrase.

We could learn from Adam. The wife says, "You're putting on weight." He responds, "It's the McDonald's Big Mac and supersized fries you give me." Of course, that's the fast-food place he told her to go to with that specific order.

The boss says, "You were late with your paperwork and there are many errors." You respond, "The secretary you hired is too slow and can't type."

The officer says, "Driver's license and registration, please."

"Officer, I saw that you were a police officer and I did not want to hold you up, so when you came up on my bumper, I accelerated so you could get to the crime scene."

Or the classic: The state trooper asks, "Why were you speeding away from me?"

"It's your fault, officer."

"How's that?"

"You see, my wife ran off with a state trooper two years ago. I was afraid you were him and you were bringing her back."

Adam passes the buck to Eve. Eve passes it to the snake. If you are left holding the buck, then you lose. In this story, it's the snake, who apparently loses his legs and has to crawl on his belly. Actually, everybody loses in this story because Adam and Eve disobeyed. Adam has to work hard with minimal results. Eve has to submit to Adam and experience pain in childbirth. God loses his gardeners. Back to Craigslist.

Scholars call this an "etiology," a story that explains why things are the way they are. Apparently even millennia ago, kids asked lots of "why" questions.

"Daddy, why do snakes crawl on their bellies?"

"Daddy, why did Mommy yell and scream when my little brother was being born?"

"Daddy, why do weeds and thistles grow better than anything we plant?"

"Daddy, why are you the head of the house when Mommy is smarter than you?"

"Daddy, why . . ."

And so we answer, "Son, once upon a time God planted a garden . . ."

12
Lord and Tailor

The man named his wife Eve, because she was the mother
of all living. And the Lord God made garments of skins
for the man and for his wife, and clothed them.
Then the Lord God said, "See, the man has become like one
of us, knowing good and evil; and now, he might reach
out his hand and take also from the tree of life, and eat,
and live forever"— therefore the Lord God sent him forth
from the garden of Eden, to till the ground from which
he was taken. He drove out the man; and at the east of
the garden of Eden he placed the cherubim, and a sword
flaming and turning to guard the way to the tree of life.

Gen. 3:20–24

arlier in our story, Adam had given his wife
the name "woman."

What did your father call your mother? My dad addressed Mom by her first name. But I've met men over the years who referred to their wives as "Mother." My grandfather did that. I never knew whether he was talking about his mother, his wife, or my mother. I've known men who referred to their wives as "The Wife," "Wifey," and commonly (not advisedly), "The Old Lady."

We can imagine Eve's complaint, "Why do you call me 'woman'? I hate that word."

Adam counters, "But it's part of the poem I wrote for you. You said you loved it."

"I think it was sweet that you wrote me a poem. But the name needs some work."

"Several of the animals complained about their names, too. So, how about if I just call you *wife*?"

"Come on, honey, you can be more creative than that."

And so Adam calls her "Eve" (*Havah* in Hebrew) meaning "life." She may have been the life of the party, but the party was over. Earlier, Adam and Eve had sewn loincloths out of fig leaves. Maybe that's why God does not kill them. God laughs so hard at their fig-leaf wardrobe malfunction, He does not have the heart to follow through on the original threat. I cannot imagine what a fig-leaf loincloth feels like after a couple of days as the leaves dry out. Can't you see God chuckling and saying to them, "Eating from the tree of knowledge surely did not help your fashion sense. How are those fig leaf girdles working out for you?"God graciously designs and makes garments out of animal skins for them, thus becoming their Lord and tailor.

There is a story of an elderly single Sunday school teacher who finally fulfilled her dream of going to the Holy Land. When the Israeli guide pointed out the fig tree, she said, "There must be a mistake."

The guide asked why she thought that. She responded, "I thought the leaves would surely be bigger."

After the man and the woman each strut down the catwalk and God is satisfied with their new look, God acknowledges that they have become like God, knowing good and evil. The snake was right after all. But this creates a problem. Apparently, God is ready for the empty nest. If the man and woman eat from the tree of life, they will live forever. The Divine Father will never get rid of His children. God is worried. Apparently, He has been looking forward to getting the kids out of the house. Maybe you have been there when company stayed too long. Like Moses later in the Bible. Jethro (his future father-in-law) invites Moses over for dinner. He stayed 40 years.

God drives man and woman out of the garden and posts a guard with a flaming, twirling sword to keep them out. God cannot keep them innocent any longer, but God can keep them mortal and keep them out.

Some parents give their kids luggage on their 18th birthday. The teenagers understand that graduation from high school means they are expected to leave. Parents may not post a guard, but the kids get the idea. When the teenager comes back from the prom, there is a billiard table where his bed had been. On the table there is a note saying, "We enjoyed your visit. Tomorrow morning you have an appointment at O600 at the recruiter's office. Have a nice life."

Of course, the moral of the biblical story is that we are mortal. Many preachers have lamented the first couple's eating the forbidden fruit and thus coming to know both good and evil. Thereby humanity lost its innocence. But my complaint is that the first couple got so distracted trying to sew fig-leaf outfits when they should have made a beeline to the tree of life. Think about it. We could have been both informed and immortal. Wouldn't it be great to be like God, living forever, not growing old, not dying? No need for Oil of Olay or Ben-Gay. In time we could learn everything. All they had to do is eat from the tree of life in the middle of the garden. Eating from the pomegranate tree of the knowledge of good and evil did not make them smart enough to eat from the banana tree of eternal life.

Apparently, we were not created to live forever.

13
God Is Not a Vegetarian

Now the man knew his wife Eve, and she conceived and bore Cain, saying, "I have produced a man with the help of the Lord." Next she bore his brother Abel. Now Abel was a keeper of sheep, and Cain a tiller of the ground. In the course of time Cain brought to the Lord an offering of the fruit of the ground, and Abel for his part brought of the firstlings of his flock, their fat portions. And the Lord had regard for Abel and his offering, but for Cain and his offering he had no regard. So Cain was very angry, and his countenance fell. The Lord said to Cain, "Why are you angry, and why has your countenance fallen? If you do well, will you not be accepted? And if you do not do well, sin is lurking at the door; its desire is for you, but you must master it."

Cain said to his brother Abel, "Let us go out to the field."
And when they were in the field, Cain rose up against his
brother Abel, and killed him. Then the Lord said to Cain,
"Where is your brother Abel?" He said, "I do not know; am
I my brother's keeper? And the Lord said, "What have you
done? Listen; your brother's blood is crying out to me from
the ground! And now you are cursed from the ground,
which has opened its mouth to receive your brother's blood
from your hand. When you till the ground, it will no
longer yield to you its strength; you will be a fugitive and
a wanderer on the earth."

Genesis 4:1-12

Why does God accept Abel's sacrifice and not Cain's? It's simple. God is not a vegetarian. Apologies to all vegans and vegetarians, but God prefers meat.

The ancient people thought that they were feeding gods with their sacrifices. At the end of one of the Ancient Near East flood stories (nearly every culture had one), the hero offers an animal sacrifice (like Noah) and the text says, "the gods gathered like flies." Why?

They were hungry. They had not eaten during the whole flood event.

Israelite theology is a little more sophisticated, but the background of the Hebrew Bible is that gods devoured the aroma of the sacrifices. There is nothing like the smell of steaks grilling. Who can resist the smell of barbecue? So God accepts Abel's meat offering and not Cain's grain offering.

Some have argued that Cain's offering of wheat is not much of a sacrifice on Cain's part. As a pastor I know about Cain's kind of "sacrificial" giving.

A wife and her husband are having a conversation.

"Honey, that couch in your man cave has to go. It's terrible."

"Yes, I know it's bad, but it's comfortable. Besides, it cost a fortune."

"Yes, dear, but that was 25 years ago. I can't even vacuum by it unless I'm armed with a can of air freshener. Have you ever turned on the light and actually looked at that thing?"

"Well, no. My 60-inch TV provides all the light we need down there."

"That sofa has to go."

"Okay. Then do I get the couch in the living room?"

"Why, that's a brilliant idea. Then we can get a new sectional for the living room."

"What are we going to do with my man-cave couch?"

"Let's put it on the curb for the garbage collectors to pick up."

"I have a better idea. Let's donate it to the church for the youth."

"Great idea."

"Then we can get a tax write-off too. As a donation to the church, it's worth at least $5,000. And the youth will love it."

I know what some Christians will be sitting on in heaven—the furniture they donated to the church for the youth group.

Firstlings of Abel's flock were clearly more valuable than a grain offering. Because Abel offers only the "fat portions" of the animals, the whole family would have enjoyed the rest of the barbecued meat.

As they are doing the dishes after the picnic, Eve says, "Cain's vegetable tray was nice, but Abel's steaks were to die for."

It reminds me of the story of Bubba and his neighbors. Every Friday night after work, Bubba would fire up his outdoor grill and cook steaks. But all of Bubba's neighbors were Catholic, and since it was Lent, they were forbidden from eating meat on Friday. The delicious aroma from the grilled steaks was causing such a problem for the Catholic faithful, they finally complained to their priest.

The priest came to visit Bubba and suggested that he become a Catholic. After several classes and much study, Bubba attended Mass. The priest sprinkled holy water over him and said, "You were born a Baptist, and raised a Baptist, but now you are a Catholic."

Bubba's neighbors were greatly relieved, until Friday night arrived and the wonderful aroma of grilled steaks filled the neighborhood.

The neighbors complained to their priest again. The priest went to Bubba's house walked around to the backyard, fully prepared to scold him.

But when he saw him, he stopped and watched in amazement. There stood Bubba, clutching a small bottle of holy water which he carefully sprinkled over the grilling beef and chanted: "You wuz born a cow, you wuz raised a cow, but now you is a catfish."[iv]

Cain is angry that God does not accept his sacrifice. But how does he know? Does God come down and put a "First Place" blue ribbon on Abel's sacrifice and a "Participant" ribbon on Cain's? Does God send fire on Abel's and not his brother's?

We don't know, but somehow Cain knows that God prefers his baby brother's offering.

Cain is not just angry over the sacrifice. Like many firstborn children, Cain has experienced "dethronement" because everybody loves the baby—even God.

And Cain is fed up with it.

God said—*If you do well, you will be accepted.* Don't we *all* want to be accepted? Being born first got Cain

---

iv   Source unknown.

accepted in the beginning, but when his little brother was born, Abel became the center of attention.

I was the firstborn. So I was the star—until my younger siblings came along, which was fairly soon. I can't remember being a solo star, but I can remember feeling something of mine had been taken or had to be shared.

"Look at him. He learns so much faster than Cain did. Wow! He's walking at nine months. Cain, you didn't walk until you were almost a year old. And Abel said complete sentences long before you did. He's so athletic. Look at him climb."

"You never let me climb the furniture like that," Cain complains.

So the firstborn lives in the shadow of the younger. Shadows are dark places.

I never resented my brother Joe, who came along 14 months after I did. Just because he passed me in size when I was five and everyone thought he was the oldest, I didn't hold it against him. Just because he was intellectually gifted and a mechanical genius … I was not jealous. In no way did I resent giving up my "star" spot to him. Then, along came another baby brother, and—even worse—a baby sister. I was long forgotten.

My only hope was that I got to go to school first so I could excel. So I worked hard and did well. I remember the first time I got straight A's on my report card. My brother Joe had been getting B's and a C or two. Mom knew he could do better. She challenged him. Without bringing home books, Joe managed to get A's and B's the next grading period. Mom bragged about him.

I said, "Yeah. But look I got straight A's." Nothing competitive about me.

Mom dismissed my accomplishment saying, "You always make good grades." I was crushed. If my good grades meant nothing, how could I shine?

I understand Cain. I have lived in the shadows.

Cain thinks, "You think you are so special. I was here first. I wanted a puppy, not a baby brother. Mom and Dad didn't listen to me. Why did they need another boy? They had one already. When you came along, they forgot all about me. They let you get away with things I never got to do. I was told we were vegetarians. So they taught me to grow crops. Then you came along, and the rules change. They put you in charge of the animals and you open Baby Boy's Barbecue. It's not fair. It's never been fair since you came along. It's my world—not yours."

Then Cain says to Abel, "Hey, little brother, let's go for a walk."

God warns Cain that sin is crouching at the door.

I admit, I've heard sin scratching at the door from time to time.

"Hey, Joe, let's go for a walk."

14
Noah Names His Kids

*When Lamech had lived one hundred eighty-two years,
he became the father of a son; he named him Noah, saying,
"Out of the ground that the Lord has cursed this one shall
bring us relief from our work and from the toil of our
hands." Lamech lived after the birth of Noah five hundred
ninety-five years, and had other sons and daughters. Thus
all the days of Lamech were seven hundred seventy-seven
years; and he died.
After Noah was five hundred years old, Noah became the
father of Shem, Ham, and Japheth.*

Genesis 5:28-32

Noah was not particularly creative. How
do we know that? Look at the names he
gave his sons: Shem, Ham, and Japheth. Shem means
"Name."

Picture it, if you will: Mrs. Noah is expecting her first. She and Noah are at Lamaze class. Mrs. Noah is practicing her breathing. She asks the father-to-be, "What name have you picked out?"

"Still working on it," he responds.

Several months later, she says, "The baby is coming. Have you *finally* come up with a name?"

There is a logical reason for the question. For one thing, our man Noah was 500 years old before he became a father.

Maybe Noah was not so quick in a lot of ways.

So he says, "Name? Name? That's it," Noah says. "What about Name?"

She says, "You want to name our baby Name?"

"Name. And that's my final answer." And so Noah names his first child "Name" (Shem).

Then look at what he names his second son—Ham. Who names a Jewish kid "Ham"? *Really*? Don't you think the other kids are going to make fun of him? You can just hear the bacon jokes even after all these years.

For the third child, Noah tries to plan ahead. So he's looking at his wife in the weeks before she gives birth and comes up with the name "Japheth" which means "Getting Bigger." Perhaps she'd gained more weight with the last one. Kind of makes you wonder if this choice of names made Mrs. Noah so upset, she moved to the other bedroom?

"No more kids for you, mister," she tells him. "I hate to think what you would name the next one—Water Broke or Stretch Marks or maybe Play Centa."

Well, now you know why Noah and his wife only had the three sons.

15
Heavenly Affairs

*When people began to multiply on the face of the ground,
and daughters were born to them, the sons of God saw
that they were fair; and they took wives for themselves of
all that they chose. Then the Lord said, "My spirit shall
not abide in mortals forever, for they are flesh; their days
shall be one hundred twenty years." The Nephilim were on
the earth in those days—and also afterward—when the
sons of God went in to the daughters of humans, who bore
children to them. These were the heroes that were of old,
warriors of renown.*

Genesis 6:1-4

This is a strange passage in the Bible. People
are multiplying. In other words, we are
obeying that one command we got right: be fruitful
and multiply. That part seems clear enough. Then it

gets a little bizarre. In human reproduction, daughters are born as well as sons. Imagine that! And some of these young women are drop-dead gorgeous. The "sons of God" see they are attractive and take wives from the good-looking ones.

What I want to know is this: was this the first Miss Universe Pageant?

Oddly enough, there are two beauty contests in the Bible. The first (if we exclude this one) involves King David. Near the end of his life, David can't keep warm in bed, even when buried in wool blankets. So his servants hold a beauty contest. Apparently, they are thinking that a beautiful young woman would get his motor running. Warm him up a bit. Even though the king is old, he still has standards and apparently Bathsheba can't warm him up any more. Perhaps all the young women in his harem have aged out.

Which leads me to wonder: what was the mandatory retirement age for King David's harem—twenty-three?

What do they tell these young women to get them to compete in the beauty contest? "You'll dine at the King's table; the best cuisine every day. You'll never have to work a day in your life. Instead, you'll adorn yourself with the world's finest perfumes and oils … relax in the luxurious royal spas and enjoy daily massages."

A gorgeous young Shunammite virgin wins the contest. Her prize? Yes, she gets to live in the palace. But *bigger* surprise! "Honey, you get to climb in bed with the most powerful man in the Middle East, a warrior among warriors, a king of kings. Your service to your king is simple—keep him warm at night."

In other words, jump in bed with a shriveled-up 70-year-old man, who shivers constantly because his body is as cold as ice, who suffers from erectile dysfunction, and is near death.[v]

Not exactly a crown and a bouquet of roses, but I suppose taking care of (up to then) Israel's greatest king is prize enough.

The second beauty pageant happens in the Book of Esther. King Ahasuerus, the king of Persia, becomes enraged with his Queen Vashti when she refuses to appear before his drunken frat party. He banishes her from the palace. Then he holds a beauty contest. He puts all the best candidates in his harem. In preparation the young women marinate in beauty oils for six months. The talent portion of that contest includes spending a night with the king. Esther apparently has the best "act" so he declares her to be his new queen.[vi]

Was this how the "sons of God" picked the most attractive? What about all the other ladies? I feel sorry for them. Was *this* the beginning of wearing veils in the Ancient Near East?

Or maybe the story from Genesis, unlike the stories from Kings and Esther, was not that organized.

---

v   I Kings 1:1-4.
vi   Esther 2:1-18

Perhaps whenever one of God's sons in heaven saw a young woman he liked, he would swoop down in a flaming chariot and take her back to heaven. Do they do that kind of thing in heaven? Or was the heavenly being forced to stay on earth? Could they then go back and forth?

Maybe heaven's boys showed up in groups, sort of like a celestial motorcycle gang rolling into town. They picked the prettiest women to be their biker chicks. The women hopped on the seats and held on for dear life as they thundered off into the sunset.

Can't you just see the non-son-of-God nerd standing on the sidewalk near the front door? He has her prom corsage in one hand and a bouquet in the other. He's practicing his line, "Good evening. You look beautiful." Then he hears the roar of the Harley. He spins to see his date on the backseat of the motorcycle, with her prom dress hiked up as she straddles behind this huge heavenly biker guy. They roar away.

Perhaps rumors of these heavenly dudes started circulating through the high school. Cheerleaders were no longer trying to impress the football players on the field. They start shaking their pompoms heavenward.

"Two-four-six-eight. Who do we appreciate? A heavenly date. A heavenly date."

All of this created problems, including incredible longevity. We assume that the "sons of God" were immortal. What happened when an immortal, to use the biblical language, "came into" an earthly female? Was the offspring immortal? Apparently God couldn't control the boys from heaven, but he put a limit on human life span—one hundred twenty years. (Interestingly enough, modern gerontologists say that the maximum human life span is 120 years.)

Was this because the first divine/human offspring were living tens of thousands of years? Or is this a reference to those humans who apparently had normal human fathers, like Adam and Seth, who were only living 800 and 900 years?

God decides to put term limits on human life. But in the ensuing chapters it takes a while for this limit to take effect. Even though Adam and Eve do not eat from the Tree of Life, they must brush up against it, because their descendants live long lives.

God gets tired of it. We are told that a thousand years is like a day to God (Psalm 90:4; 2 Peter 3:8). So what's this problem of human longevity like from God's eternal perspective? "Okay, kids, I let you stay up an hour past your bedtime. It's time to put you to sleep. I mean, go to sleep."

Apparently one characteristic of the divine/human descendants is that they were giants. (Was this when C-sections became necessary?)

Now, what about the daughters of God? Wouldn't they be miffed that the sons got to sow their wild oats while they were stuck in heaven fluffing feathers, tuning harps and polishing halos (or whatever the daughters of God do)?

At some point, did the sons of God get banned from visiting the celestial sorority sisters? If their visits produced giants on the earth, did it mean no angel babies were born in heaven during this time? Were they cut off from celestial conjugal visits?

Could the daughters of God tell if the sons of God had been with an earthling beauty? "I have a headache. Besides, you smell of earth, my dear."

I'm just glad the "sons of God" did not visit my high school. Now that I think about it, that is who the basketball players told the cheerleaders they were ...

... and the girls said those boys were *divine*.

16
First Father's Day

The Lord saw that the wickedness of humankind was great in the earth, and that every inclination of the thoughts of their hearts was only evil continually. And the Lord was sorry that he had made humankind on the earth, and it grieved him to his heart. So the Lord said, "I will blot out from the earth the human beings I have created—people together with animals and creeping things and birds of the air, for I am sorry that I have made them." But Noah found favor in the sight of the Lord.

These are the descendants of Noah. Noah was a righteous man, blameless in his generation; Noah walked with God. And Noah had three sons, Shem, Ham, and Japheth.

Genesis 6:5-10

When was Father's Day first celebrated? It must have happened on the Ark. When

Mrs. Noah, their sons and daughters-in-law realize they are spared because of righteous Noah, party time ensues. The sons say, "Dad, thanks for keeping everything above board with us." Mrs. Noah says, "I'm so glad I married you, honey, even though my parents were worried you would not provide for us. But look at us now. The ark is paid for and everyone else is underwater."

God has had it with humans. He is fed up with all of them—that is, except Noah. Is it because God has been too lenient? God did not execute Cain when he murdered his brother, but instead made him a wanderer. The Lord did not kill Adam and Eve when they ate the forbidden fruit even though the Lord had threatened they would die on the very day. Instead God made them a new wardrobe and *then* evicted them from paradise.

God reminds me of myself as a father. My wife was the consistent disciplinarian. Not me. I'd threaten to ground my son for a month, then not actually do it. When my son's defiance escalated, I tended to lose my temper and say things like, "I brought you into this world and I can take you out." Not that I ever would.

Is this where God is in this story? God had thousands of oppositional children. They openly rebelled. Has God lost it and is now ready to kill everyone? Apparently not.

God's emotion here is not wrath but grief. It's one of the saddest lines in the Bible—*And the Lord was sorry that he had made humankind on the earth, and it grieved him to his heart.* God has moved past anger. God concludes that people are always inclined to evil thoughts, which lead to evil actions. It is sadness and grief that prompt God's death sentence on humanity.

I wonder if God is still sad.

God is fond of Noah. They used to take walks together. (How fast do you have to walk to keep up with God?) But why does God like Noah so much? Noah is said to be blameless; how can a person be blameless?

(Have no fear; I discovered the secret.) Noah never spoke.

Well, he did speak once, but it was after the flood and after he had gotten drunk then woke with a bad hangover (more about that later).

That's the secret to being blameless—not ever talking. God says, "Build a boat, Noah." Noah does not ask questions. He builds a boat. God says, "Make it three hundred cubits long, fifty cubits wide and thirty cubits high." Noah does not even ask, "What's a cubit?"

God says the flood will blot out all humans except for Noah and his family. We want Noah to say something here. Please tell me that Noah pleads with God not to destroy all the earth. We want to see him bargain with God, "Merciful God, if you find 50 righteous people, will you still destroy everyone?"

That's what Abraham does later on when trying to change God's mind about destroying Sodom. Abraham starts with 50 but bargains God down to ten. If there are just ten righteous people in Sodom, God promises not to destroy it (Genesis 18:16-33).

But Noah never speaks. He pulls the cord on his neighbor's chainsaw and starts cutting down trees. Why doesn't he question God about one of his neighbors possibly being worth saving? Maybe the guy who loaned him the chainsaw? Could he not advocate for humanity?

On the other hand, so often it is when we open our mouths that we get in trouble. At least that has been my experience. The quiet kids are the good kids—just ask any teacher or parent. They are compliant and still. They are the easy kids.

When I was twelve years old, I told a joke—which, by the way, my father had told me—to the whole Boy Scout troop and all the parents at the closing campfire after a week of camping. I thought it was funny. My father was a deacon in the Baptist church. It never occurred to me that it was *not* the kind of joke that one tells in mixed company. My words embarrassed my father and the troop leader, whose judgment was swift. I had to eat a bar of soap. Listening to a kid gagging on soap behind a tent had to be worse than the joke—seriously.

The editor of Genesis would have us believe that the blameless never speak but simply obey God. My mother favored this kind of righteousness. Mom's favorite lines were:

"Children should be seen and not heard."

"Do as you are told."

"Don't ask why, just do it." (A line stolen by Nike, by the way.)

"Because I said so."

"This is not a democracy. You don't get to vote."

Her favorite proverb was: "Be silent and be thought a fool. Open your mouth and remove all doubt."

I would not have made a very good Noah. Blameless men are rare. Job is also called blameless at the beginning of that book in the Bible (Job 1:1), but that's before God allows Satan to take everything away from Job and afflicts him with sores from head to sole. It is also before Job starts complaining about his plight and calling God unjust and unfair, which goes on for many chapters (Job 3-38). Eventually Job repents of all his complaints and accusations against God (Job 40:3-4, 42:1-6). Fortunately for Job, God still likes him in the end and gives him twice as many sheep, oxen, camels, and donkeys as Job had before he lost everything (Job 42:10-12).

It pays to be blameless. Just ask Noah—but don't expect an answer.

17
Aboard the First Cruise Ship

In the six hundredth year of Noah's life, in the second month, on the seventeenth day of the month, on that day all the fountains of the great deep burst forth, and the windows of the heavens were opened. The rain fell on the earth forty days and forty nights. On the very same day Noah with his sons, Shem and Ham and Japheth, and Noah's wife and the three wives of his sons entered the ark, they and every wild animal of every kind, and all domestic animals of every kind, and every creeping thing that creeps on the earth, and every bird of every kind— every bird, every winged creature. They went into the ark with Noah, two and two of all flesh in which there was

the breath of life. And those that entered, male and female
of all flesh, went in as God had commanded him; and the
Lord shut him in.

Genesis 7:11-16

We might think of Noah's ark as a cargo ship, carrying the world's first zoo, but what if the ark is the first cruise ship? The animals have their assigned tables for every meal as a necessary precaution. You can almost hear the conversation that occurs when Mrs. Lion asks Mrs. Tiger, "What do you think Mr. and Mrs. Hyena were laughing so much about last night in their cabin?"

Mrs. Tiger volunteers, "I don't know, but I'll tell you this much: they have the cabin just above us and they were quite loud."

"Uh-oh. Do you think there will be hyena cubs soon?" asks Mrs. Lion.

"Oh, who cares what those dogs do?" retorts Mrs. Tiger. "I'm more interested in the rabbits. Have you heard? After three months there are already 38 rabbits on board."

"That's good news. I'm growing weary of this vegetarian diet," says Mrs. Lion.

"Captain Noah said he would have the chef prepare roasted rabbit for us when we dine at the captain's table tomorrow," Mrs. Tiger informs.

Meanwhile, "Why do Mrs. Tiger and Mrs. Lion keep staring at us," asks Little Rabbit No. 35.

Baby Rabbit No. 27 hops over to a table where Mrs. Field Mouse is crying inconsolably. She complains to all the mice at her table, "My last litter just disappeared from our nest in the middle of the night. They were almost full grown. How could that happen?"

Mr. Field Mouse says, "I talked with Captain Noah and he informed me that in our cruise-ship contract, the cruise line is only responsible for the original male and female of each species. There's nothing he can do."

Meanwhile, the Wolves and the Foxes dine with Mr. and Mrs. Noah at the captain's table. Mr. Wolf swallows a spoonful of stew. He smiles and says, "There seems to be a bit more protein in tonight's fare."

Mrs. Noah intones, "You are beneficiaries of rapid rodent reproductive cycles."

Noah says, "Let's keep our voice down, dear. We don't want to disturb any of our other guests."

Before dessert is served, Shem runs up to the table to report a problem. "The hippos," he says, "are hogging the pool. Meanwhile … the alligators are hissing and threatening to take legal action."

Noah says, "But isn't it still raining outside? And exactly what are they doing in the pool?"

Shem hesitates. "I don't know if I should say this in mixed company, but the hippos said something about chafing and that the rain wasn't reaching their 'lower decks'."

Mr. Wolf laughs. "I was only out there twenty minutes this morning and all my decks were swamped. You can't even see the mountaintops any more—only water. And the hippos want more?"

"Good luck to the alligators on finding a lawyer," volunteers Mr. Fox. "The last firm in town went under two weeks ago."

"Oh, but I saw a lawyer hanging on the side of the ark yesterday," Mrs. Wolf adds. "We had a pleasant conversation."

Noah asks, "Really? I'm surprised the sharks hadn't eaten him."

Mrs. Wolf responds, "I asked him about the sharks. He said they didn't bother him—" She shrugs. "Something about professional courtesy."

18
Noah Opened a Window

At the end of forty days Noah opened the window of the ark that he had made and sent out the raven; and it went to and fro until the waters were dried up from the earth. Then he sent out the dove from him, to see if the waters had subsided from the face of the ground; but the dove found no place to set its foot, and it returned to him to the ark, for the waters were still on the face of the whole earth. So he put out his hand and took it and brought it into the ark with him. He waited another seven days, and again he sent out the dove from the ark; and the dove came back to him in the evening, and there in its beak was a freshly plucked olive leaf; so Noah knew that the waters had subsided from the earth. Then he waited another seven

*days, and sent out the dove; and it did not return to
him anymore.*

Genesis 8:6-12

I'm convinced Noah had sinus issues. How else do you explain one of the funniest lines in the Bible? "At the end of forty days Noah opened the window of the ark that he had made." But wait! Forty days was on top of the nine months he has been cooped up with one pair of all living things, three sons, three daughters-in-law and his wife. So after more than ten months he *finally* opens a window? The ark was a big boat, but it wasn't *that* big. He must have been afflicted with some kind of olfactory dysfunction.

Do you ever wonder what size litter box do you need for a 900-pound Siberian tiger? What do you do with the waste that a 14,000-pound elephant produces daily?

How long would it take for Noah's sons (and/or their wives) to muck out so many stalls? Did they invent the "bucket and chuck it" method for waste removal before the Environmental Protection Agency banned the practice?

Is it Mrs. Noah who says she will go crazy unless Noah does something about the vile stench?

"Gosh, we have been cooped up here so long, I forgot about the windows," says Noah.

Of course, opening a window is also part of Noah's bird experiment. He has a minor in ornithology and always wanted to experiment with behavior patterns of winged creatures. His first attempt at bird behavior is with the raven. Of course, his practical purpose is obvious. The cruise ship is grounded high in the Ararat Mountains. Noah does not want to disembark until he knows the ground is dry enough for him to plant his vineyard.

When he releases the raven, it does not return. Short experiment. Then he releases a dove, which returns to him. He waits a week and, once again, sends out the dove and it returns again. Noah begins to have fun with his new hobby.

"Hey, honey. Watch this." He opens the window and tosses the dove up in the air. It flies away.

She is not impressed, "All the birds would leave if you let them go."

Noah says, "Wait for it. Wait for it."

At that moment the dove comes gliding back and lands on Noah's wrist. Mrs. Noah is not paying attention because she is too busy sucking in the fresh air from the open window.

Another week goes by and again he repeats the experiment. This time the dove comes back with a leaf in its beak.

Noah is so excited, he tells his wife, "Not only did she come back, she brought me a present!"

However, when he releases the dove the following week, it does not return. Noah becomes depressed. He really had grown to love his pet dove.

I wonder if Noah did not want to get off the boat because he wanted to stay captain of the ship and ruler of the zoo. As long as he remained on the boat, he was in charge of all animal life on the planet. What would happen when he opened the doors? Chaos? They had developed their routine on the ark, and it would be difficult to leave it.

19
Graduation Day

*In the six hundred first year, in the first month, the first
day of the month, the waters were dried up from the
earth; and Noah removed the covering of the ark, and
looked, and saw that the face of the ground was drying.
In the second month, on the twenty-seventh day of the
month, the earth was dry. Then God said to Noah, "Go out
of the ark, you and your wife, and your sons and your sons'
wives with you. Bring out with you every living thing
that is with you of all flesh—birds and animals and every
creeping thing that creeps on the earth—so that they may
abound on the earth, and be fruitful and multiply on the
earth." So Noah went out with his sons and his wife and
his sons' wives. And every animal, every creeping thing,
and every bird, everything that moves on the earth, went
out of the ark by families.*

Genesis 8:13-19

After a year, Noah removed the covering
of the ark, which surely allowed a huge
methane cloud to escape—a cloud so large it impacted
the ozone layer around the earth, and for the next six
months rainbows appeared.

Even with more space on deck, Captain Noah has to come up with a schedule so that the animals will not fight over the deck chairs. This way everyone has a chance for a good tan before they depart the cruise ship. They all get their day in the sun, and vitamin D deficiencies are remedied.

In the beginning not all the animals had been happy on the ark. In fact, the gorillas, the bison, the lions and many others had been furious to be cooped up instead of roaming free. Most of the animals, including the white-tailed deer, the gazelles, and the koalas, had been terrified at being confined against their will. But in time, the disgruntled cruisers have warmed up to Noah and his family and even see them as their rescuers—a psychological phenomenon known as Stockyard Syndrome, which is a zoological version of Stockholm Syndrome.

God finally has to tell Noah to get off the ark. Again we see Noah's passive obedience. Wouldn't most people have been asking God, "Are we there yet? Can't we get off this boat? Isn't it time? How much longer? How long, O Lord?" But Noah is in no hurry to be "de-captained" and return to living off the land.

After a year on the ship, Captain & Mrs. Noah decide to award diplomas to each family for having survived Ark Academy, also known as the best survival school on the planet. As with most graduating classes, they vote on members to receive different honors.

Miss Bunny wins Miss Popularity. It seems everyone from the greyhounds to the panthers were chasing after her. Mr. Cockroach is voted Most Likely to Succeed although he had complained about a *raid* on his nest. The Homecoming King and Queen titles go to chimpanzee twins who'd been born on the ark. Mr. Gecko is awarded the biggest scholarship in marketing and advertising, which will save him 15% or more. Mrs. Orangutan gives the valedictorian speech.

As each family of animals walks down the ramp, they are introduced. "We congratulate Mr. & Mrs. White Rhinoceros and their cute twin rhinos, Stubby and Priscilla. Having completed all the requirements of the Ark Academy Survival School, we award you this diploma."

Then Mrs. Noah makes some personal comments. "While there were accusations of Mrs. White Rhinoceros sticking her nose into other people's business, I'm sure we can agree she always had a point."

Down the ramp they come to the applause and cheers of all the other animals. Captain Noah concludes the comments for each family with the instructions, "Be fruitful and multiply and fill the earth." That will make the male animals smile, and the females call for Bayer Aspirin as they lead their little ones off the ark.

As each family disembarks, Japheth photographs them, which causes a backup getting off the ship, especially when the peacock family insists on dozens of poses. Of course, the sloths take their time. Some families want the deluxe package, which includes shots of the family on deck holding umbrellas while Shem sprays water down on them. Another favorite is the dad holding one of the little ones over the side of the ark by a leg.

Ham sells the portrait packages at the bottom of the ramp.

After the formalities, they hold a huge picnic where families take turns at the microphone to tell what they enjoyed most about the cruise. The greyhounds say it was chasing the rabbits. The hippos enjoyed the pool. The seagulls and the kookaburras note the comedy club. The spider monkeys say their kids had liked swinging from stall to stall, which brings a roar from the lions.

Mr. Mouse jumps up on the podium and thanks the dessert chef for naming his famous chocolate mousse after their family, which causes the Moose family to stampede toward the podium asserting that the dessert was actually named in their honor.

Lots of games go on all afternoon. The corn hole game generates lots of laughter until the Rottweiler pups run off with the bean bags. The three-legged race has to be modified, but the cheetahs still win in the end.

Noah asks the wolf cub to blow up the balloons, but after only three balloons he complains of too much huffing and puffing. The pig triplets volunteer but they seem to have a taste for the rubber.

Noah's sons can't find a ball for dodgeball so they ask the younger porcupine to roll himself up. When that doesn't work out, they looked for the hedgehog family, who by now have decided Hide-n-Seek is a better game for them. On the far left side of the field, the giraffe siblings are busy winning the hula hoop competition, while a few yards away, horses protest the horseshoe toss as being insensitive and politically incorrect.

The piñata does not work out so well when the silverback gorilla knocks the piñata to the other side of Mount Ararat. Only the mountain goats are able to get some of the candy, while the zebras, goats, and gazelles enjoy a game of Twister ... that is, until the anaconda asked to join in.

Ham pins a huge map of the earth on a bulletin board. Families enjoy pinning their photos to the map to show where they are relocating. The pandas put their photo on Asia and the polar bears attach theirs to the Arctic. The reindeer note that they will not reside at the North Pole, as had been rumored, but in the wintry regions of North America, Greenland, Europe, and Asia. The jaguars place their photo in the jungles of South America. The head of the platypus family keeps asking for someone to show him the *exact* location of "down under."

Everyone everywhere takes out their iPhones for selfies with Captain & Mrs. Noah, showing the ark in the background. The elephants get creative and take photos of their twins with their trunks in the air and the ark in the background so it appears they are holding up the ark.

Just before sundown Captain Noah bids everyone a sad farewell. Then Mrs. Noah and her daughters-in-law (who had formed the Ark Ladies Quartet) sing "I Hope You Dance," which brings both smiles and tears to everyone.

The animals who had come in by twosies-twosies so seemingly long ago, exchange phone numbers and email addresses and promise to stay in touch before saying their farewells.

But things never are the same again between humans and animals ... especially after Noah opens his chain of steakhouses.

20
Grilling for God

Then Noah built an altar to the Lord, and took of every
clean animal and of every clean bird, and offered burnt
offerings on the altar. And when the Lord smelled the
pleasing odor, the Lord said in his heart, "I will never
again curse the ground because of humankind, for the
inclination of the human heart is evil from youth; nor will
I ever again destroy every living creature as I have done.
As long as the earth endures,
seedtime and harvest, cold and heat,
summer and winter, day and night,
shall not cease."

Genesis 8:20-22

As mentioned earlier, in the ancient world the gods were fed by savoring the aroma of sacrifices. What was it like for God to go more than a year without nourishment? Was God, at this point, famished? Perhaps it would be like a member of Weight Watchers who takes a year to reach her goal weight and decides to reward herself with a "death by chocolate" dessert, gaining back five pounds at her next weigh-in. Then again, if you are nourished by smelling the aroma of barbecued beef offered in sacrifice, maybe gaining weight is not a problem. My mother used to claim that when she cooked all those big meals for the family, she gained weight just by smelling the food.

God reacts to the sacrifice in a positive way—sort of. God is enjoying savoring the aromas of the grill so much, He says, "What was I thinking? I really have missed this. No, not going to do that flood thing again. Even though these people are always thinking up evil, I'll let them carry on. Oh, how I have missed this barbecue!"

Was God's goal in the flood to kill off all the evil people and start over with righteous Noah and his family? Apparently, even though Noah has not yet gotten drunk and actually cursed his grandson (yeah, this is coming), God realizes humans may be a lost cause ... but, at the same time, we do cook a mean steak.

But has God resigned himself to the reality of human evil?

A woman and her grandmother, a very forgiving and religious soul, sat on their porch discussing a member of the family. "He's just no good," the young woman said. "He's completely untrustworthy, not to mention lazy."

"Yes, he's bad," the grandmother said as she rocked back and forth in her rocker, "but Jesus loves him."

"I'm not so sure of that," the younger woman persisted.

"Oh, yes," assured the elderly lady. "Jesus loves him."

She rocked and thought a few more minutes and then added, "Of course, Jesus doesn't know him like we do . . ."

However, in our biblical passage God *does* appear to know us. Do we agree with God's assessment? Sure, we may have in an inclination to evil, but we don't always give in. (I do turn down dessert, sometimes.)

It's interesting to see how biases affect translators. The NRSV is an accurate translation of the phrase *for the inclination of the human heart is evil from youth.* The conservative NIV translators have something close—*even though every inclination of his heart is evil from childhood.* The word "every" does not appear in the Hebrew text. They see "every" implied because we are all born in original sin, "totally depraved," an old way of saying we are bad to the bone. I would not buy a used car from the NIV translators.

The Hebrew word is *yetser*, which is translated "inclination" in both these versions, and relates to the verb *"yatsar,"* "to form or shape," as a potter might shape clay. So our hearts (minds) have been shaped or formed with a bent toward evil. Don't we have another inclination toward good? That's what the rabbis taught, that we have a good *yetser* and a bad *yetser*. Each of us has two inclinations pulling us in opposite directions.

God made us. So, isn't this evil inclination in us God's fault? Is God like a breeder of Labrador retrievers, who leaves puppies alone in the house with his slippers, sofa pillows, and beanbag chairs? He returns home to two feet of "snow" everywhere. Then he observes that these puppies have a tendency to chew everything. But aren't retrievers bred to carry things in their mouths? Hasn't God created us in God's image to think, decide, and create? If we are a mess, aren't we God's mess?

Of course, Christian thinkers will not blame God. So if God did not create us with this evil tendency, then it must be the fault of our great, great, great . . . grandparents, Adam and Eve. Surely it was all *their* fault. They sinned and everyone has been born bad ever since, like a genetic mutation in everyone's DNA.

Rather than blame our ancestors, we should see ourselves in these biblical stories. Every morning I look in the mirror and see Adam. Like those people treading the water by the ark, and like Adam and Eve, I sometimes choose to do what I should not. Unlike Adam and Eve, I'm going with a suit rather than fig leaves.

There have been debates among Christian theologians as to whether people are born bad and cannot help but sin. I prefer the idea that we have an inclination or a tendency to choose to go our own way. Because we are created in the image of God, I agree with the rabbis that we also have a positive inclination as well. That seems to fit the stories of Genesis and my experience. I don't believe in "original sin." They've all been done before.

So just do the best you can and do what Noah did—throw a couple steaks on the barbecue grill and give thanks to God—and maybe add a little barbecue sauce.

21
The Barbecue Is Now Open

God blessed Noah and his sons, and said to them, "Be fruitful and multiply, and fill the earth. The fear and dread of you shall rest on every animal of the earth, and on every bird of the air, on everything that creeps on the ground, and on all the fish of the sea; into your hand they are delivered. Every moving thing that lives shall be food for you; and just as I gave you the green plants, I give you everything."

(Genesis 9:1-3)

Humans are quick to seize the opportunity. Shem forms the Cattle Ranchers Association. Ham organizes the Pork Producers Council. Japheth develops franchise opportunities for

Smokey Bones, Longhorn, Outback Steak House, and Red Lobster.

Terror fills the animal world with God's new pronouncement. What is God thinking?

They immediately begin work on ad campaigns to influence human behavior.

Using boards from the ark, they make billboards and post them everywhere.

"Eat More Plants!" "Think of Your Cholesterol!" "Chlorophyll Not Cholesterol!" "Where's the Beef? It's in the Beans!" "Our Pain Your (Weight) Gain!"

In their second meeting, the hog suggests, "Pork Puts on Pounds."

The wolf asks, "Is that a confession or an ad?"

The cows and goats suggest: "Milk or Meat. You can't have both."

Chickens counter with: "Fried Chickens Mean No More Eggs!"

No doubt the fish get into it with such ideas as: "We Poop Where We Swim," "Our Bones Will Stick in Your Throat," "Some Fish Are Poisonous, So Why Take a Chance?"

Others want to appeal to the compassion of humans: "The Little Mermaid Is One of Us" and "When You Find Nemo, Don't Eat Him."

The shellfish community and crustaceans suggest: "God Put a Shell On Us for a Reason: You Don't Want to Go There." The oysters add: "Eating Raw Shellfish Can Be Dangerous."

Do you wonder about the conversation the animals had, discussing how they blew it on the ark? "What were we thinking?" they ask. "Now they are looking at us dropping like flies on the food chain."

The goats turn on the cows and chickens. "You were just too friendly."

"How could we have predicted this?"

The tuna and the lobster complain, "What did *we* do?"

"It's all the fault of you carnivores!"

The lions, tigers, and jaguars roar, "How were we to know he'd take us seriously?"

And with that the meeting concludes.

Did this start with Noah's complaint? *God, you are not vegetarian. Why do we have to be?*

The hogs start the animal rights group PETA—Porkers for the Ethical Treatment of Animals, inviting all species to join. The dogs suggest a name change: AETAS—Animals for the Ethical Treatment of All Species.

"Why do you care, you're man's best friend," the pigs ask.

To which the dogs retort, "Have you ever been to Korea?"

22
Rambo Puts Down His Bow

Then God said to Noah and to his sons with him, "As for me, I am establishing my covenant with you and your descendants after you, and with every living creature that is with you, the birds, the domestic animals, and every animal of the earth with you, as many as came out of the ark. I establish my covenant with you, that never again shall all flesh be cut off by the waters of a flood, and never again shall there be a flood to destroy the earth." God said, "This is the sign of the covenant that I make between me and you and every living creature that is with you, for all future generations: I have set my bow in the clouds, and it shall be a sign of the covenant between me and the earth. When I bring clouds over the earth and the bow is seen in the clouds, I will remember my covenant that is between me and you and every living creature of all flesh; and the waters shall never again become a flood to destroy

*all flesh. When the bow is in the clouds, I will see it and
remember the everlasting covenant between God and
every living creature of all flesh that is on the earth." God
said to Noah, "This is the sign of the covenant that I have
established between me and all flesh that is on the earth."*

Genesis 9:8-17

Those of us who grew up in church have memories of the story of Noah and rainbows, an easy way to connect faith with the natural world. We see a rainbow and we remember God's covenant with all His creatures. It's a lovely image to teach children.

But the biblical story has a more violent tone than that. The bow is a war bow, as in compound bows and killing Bambi's mother (although she was killed by a gun). God has been assaulting the earth with lightning arrows in the storms that flooded the earth. Think of how many times lightning strikes can occur in a storm, remembering that it rained 40 days and 40 nights. God has been on the attack with his bow.

But God puts down his bow. This reveals a new chapter with the earth. God makes a covenant with Noah. Covenants are very important in the Bible, somewhat like business contracts, but really more like marriage vows. Both sides agree to certain terms out of their relationship. As Creator and Storm-God (in addition to his many other duties), God promises never again to go overboard.

Imagine the next big thunderstorm. The eight humans, terrified. All the animals stampede in Noah's direction, and he has to convince them that the Lord is not going to flood everything.

How do I know?

Look at the rainbow. That's God's war bow that he uses to shoot down lightning when he sends the storm. He will not to destroy the earth by flood again.

But did he sign the contract and have it notarized?

Let's just say: yes. Rambo God has retired—well, he at least agreed not to wipe out everyone again by floodwaters.

The ancients thought the proper attitude toward God was to fear him. They saw God as a warrior who could snuff you out with a quick shot of his bow. This is not Cupid; this is John Rambo. We often still think of God in that way. The other day I told a bold-faced lie in the lobby of our church. Then I laughed. Several people stepped back acting as if they expected lightning to strike me and wanted to make sure they were out of range.

Of course, I do live in the part of the country with more lightning strikes each year than anywhere else. Maybe this is not because of location. Maybe I just need reminding.

23
Hangovers Are Hell

Noah, a man of the soil, was the first to plant a vineyard.
He drank some of the wine and became drunk, and he lay
uncovered in his tent. And Ham, the father of Canaan,
saw the nakedness of his father, and told his two brothers
outside. Then Shem and Japheth took a garment, laid it on
both their shoulders, and walked backward and covered
the nakedness of their father; their faces were turned
away, and they did not see their father's nakedness. When
Noah awoke from his wine and knew what his youngest
son had done to him, he said,
"Cursed be Canaan;
lowest of slaves shall he be to his brothers."
He also said,
"Blessed by the Lord my God be Shem;
and let Canaan be his slave.
May God make space for Japheth,

and let him live in the tents of Shem;
and let Canaan be his slave."

Genesis 9:20-27

*P*erhaps Noah was smarter than I've indicated. He was the first person to plant a vineyard. So how did he make wine? Wine is not a natural product of a vineyard. *Grapes* are. Squeezing the grapes produces grape juice. So who made the wine?

Here's what I think happened: Mrs. Noah is upset that Noah spends so much time on his vineyard, thus ignoring her. She finds a bunch of grapes that Noah has harvested and left in a big wooden bucket. She steps into the bucket and thoroughly stomps them in protest of being ignored. Noah leaves those grapes alone, not wanting to acknowledge the damage she has done to his grapes and his ego. When he finally gets around to cleaning up the mess, the grape juice has fermented. He samples it and finds it tasty. He brings some wine to his wife as a peace offering. As they are drinking, making up, and making out, one thing leads to another until … they pass out together in their tent. She gets up the next morning and goes looking for a bottle of Bayer, leaving Noah to sleep it off.

That's when Ham walks by and hears his dad snoring. He peeks into his parents' tent and sees Dad in his birthday suit with a plastered smile on his ruddy face. Ham nearly dies laughing. He calls his brothers to come see their 600-year-old father in such a state. But his brothers had a different take on the scene. *Then Shem and Japheth took a garment, laid it on both their shoulders, and walked backward and covered the nakedness of their father.*

Noah wakes up and finds out what Ham has done. How? Perhaps because of the pictures Ham posted on Facebook—nothing lewd, just several of Noah's wrinkled, ear-to-ear smile and a video of his thunderous honking. The photos immediately went viral.

Noah, whose head is splitting from his hangover, tweets a curse against Ham, making him a slave to Shem, but, still hungover, he curses Canaan, the grandson. No one dares correct him.

The tabloids have a field day with the story. The headlines include: *Six-Hundred-Year-Old Man Ferments Grapes and Gets Lucky*; *Hungover Hero Harangues His Heir*; *Noah to Grandson: This, Bud Is for You—%$*^Q@+#!*; *Ham's a Peeping Tom*; *Viticulture, Vitriol, & Viagra.*

Mrs. Noah begins to bottle the wine under the label "Vino de Mont Ararat." She does quite well with a simple slogan: *Wine To Revive Your Love.*

Canaan, still stinging from the curse tweet, starts a social media campaign against *over*-age drinking— Drink No Wine After Your Time. He plasters a post stating "Wine Hastens Dementia," for which Mrs. Noah sues him.

They settle out of court.

24
Family Trees and Missing Branches

These are the descendants of Noah's sons, Shem, Ham, and Japheth; children were born to them after the flood.

The descendants of Japheth: Gomer, Magog, Madai, Javan, Tubal, Meshech, and Tiras. The descendants of Gomer: Ashkenaz, Riphath, and Togarmah. The descendants of Javan: Elishah, Tarshish, Kittim, and Rodanim. From these the coastland peoples spread. These are the descendants of Japheth in their lands, with their own language, by their families, in their nations.

The descendants of Ham: Cush, Egypt, Put, and Canaan. The descendants of Cush: Seba, Havilah, Sabtah, Raamah, and Sabteca. The descendants of Raamah: Sheba and Dedan. Cush became the father of Nimrod; he was the first on earth to become a mighty warrior. He was a mighty hunter before the Lord; therefore it is said, "Like Nimrod a mighty hunter before the Lord." The beginning of his kingdom was Babel, Erech, and Accad, all of them in the land of Shinar. From that land he went into Assyria, and built Nineveh, Rehoboth-ir, Calah, and Resen between Nineveh and Calah; that is the great city.

Genesis 10:1-12

The most important skill in understanding a biblical genealogy is to read between the lines. Family trees have gaps, but those gaps don't happen by accident. They happen for a reason, and the reason is never good. Someone is left out *on purpose.*

Notice the biblical genealogy above is not complete. For example, Japheth's sons are listed as: Gomer, Magog, Madai, Javan, Tubal, Meshech, and Tiras. But only Gomer and Javan's sons are mentioned. Why don't we hear about Magog, Madai, Tubal, Meschech and Tiras's sons, grandsons, etc.? Of course, we could assume that they did not have sons, only daughters. Families are remembered through the father. Apparently daughters don't count in genealogies.

This makes no sense to me. The father's effort in bringing a child into the world is considerably less than the mother's. The mother carries the child for nine months, gives birth, which is painful and sometimes fatal, and nurses the child. In other words, we *always* know who the mother is. But Dad? Maybe that is why it was so important to the men to make certain they got their names listed.

When I was growing up there used to be jokes about the milkman or the postman, who both made deliveries to houses when the men were off at work. Not many women in those days worked outside the home. *Mom,* we were sure of. *Dad,* sometimes not.

Yet, in the Bible the sons are remembered through the father. And that's still somewhat true in our modern culture. My nephew, who is progressive in many ways, told me recently that he and his wife were going to keep having children until they had a boy to carry on the Wright name. After two daughters, they welcomed a son, who will carry on the father, grandfather, and great-grandfather's name. I was amazed that this was still important in the 21st century.

But they do live in Kentucky, where breeding is important. Although usually only for horses.

In truth, the real reason these ancestors are missing from the biblical genealogy is the same reason I don't mention certain members of my family. If, in doing your family research, you come across horse thieves, murderers, and moonshiners, you have a tendency not to pass along that information. If you read about ancestors who were burned at the stake, guillotined, or hanged, it's probably not something you'd tell your grandkids.

On the other hand, just a tiny kernel of something good can snowball into a legend. Nimrod played first base in the Little League one year. He was not a good hitter, but managed to hit the ball once, and made it around the bases because of a series of errors on the part of the other team. Nimrod's "home run" became the basis for Babe "Nimrod" Ruth, the Baseball Legend.

Seriously, we can better understand how the legend of Nimrod came to be in the biblical record by reading between the lines.

"Cush became the father of Nimrod; he was the first on earth to become a mighty warrior." (He beat the neighbor kid up for stealing his lemonade.)

"He was a mighty hunter before the Lord." (He shot a bear in the foot. The bear lost his balance and fell backward off the cliff. Nimrod still has the rug.)

". . . therefore it is said, 'Like Nimrod a mighty hunter before the Lord.'" (He used the bear story in an ad campaign to run for city commissioner.)

"The beginning of his kingdom was Babel, Erech, and Accad, all of them in the land of Shinar." (Nimrod managed three Burger King locations.)

"From that land he went into Assyria, and built Nineveh, Rehoboth-ir, Calah, and Resen between Nineveh and Calah; that is the great city." (He did quite well; he became regional manager of Burger King.)

Telling stories about our ancestors is important. As parents we feel the need to keep them positive and make them larger than life because it helps develop our children's self-esteem. That way, they know they're from a family with heroes in it. Their family matters, so they matter. Of course, later when one of these children can't get on base, he'll need to go for therapy. So did Nimrod, not to mention what happened to Magog, Madai, Tubal . . .

25
There Goes the Neighborhood

Now the whole earth had one language and the same words. And as they migrated from the east, they came upon a plain in the land of Shinar and settled there. And they said to one another, "Come, let us make bricks, and burn them thoroughly." And they had brick for stone, and bitumen for mortar. Then they said, "Come, let us build ourselves a city, and a tower with its top in the heavens, and let us make a name for ourselves; otherwise we shall be scattered abroad upon the face of the whole earth." The Lord came down to see the city and the tower, which mortals had built. And the Lord said, "Look, they are one people, and they have all one language; and this is only the beginning of what they will do; nothing that they propose to do will now be impossible for them. Come, let us go down, and confuse their language there, so that they will not understand one another's speech." So the Lord scattered

them abroad from there over the face of all the earth, and
they left off building the city. Therefore it was called Babel,
because there the Lord confused the language of all the
earth; and from there the Lord scattered them abroad over
the face of all the earth.

Genesis 11:1-9

*T*his is another etiology, a story meant to explain
why things are the way they are.

"Dad, why do those people talk funny?"

"Well, son, it's all the fault of the Babylonians."

"Really? Why?"

"Once upon a time, all the people spoke the same language. They all got together in Babylon to build a ziggurat to heaven."

"What's a cigarette?"

"Not a cigarette, a ziggurat. It's like a pyramid with steps on it the front of it so the priests climb up and can get closer to God when they offer sacrifices."

"What kind of sacrifices?"

"Sheep, goats ... and little boys like you."

"Little boys? No way!"

"Yes, that's what they did in Babylon. Back to the story, the people build a really high ziggurat and start knocking on God's door. Or, at least, they try. God is not happy."

"No solicitation, right?"

"You learned another new vocabulary word! That's right. God gets angry with the Babylonians and confuses them so that their language sounds like *babel*. And then God scatters the people everywhere so they cannot communicate and will not build a tower to come knocking on his door again. To this day, people speak different languages so we cannot understand each other because of those Babylonians!"

In the story from our biblical selection, humans are all working together to make a name for themselves. Whom are they trying to impress? The animals? The gods? There are no other humans. They are concerned about being scattered.

This is the ancient storyteller's way of giving away the ending. Ancients did not like the drama of suspense as we do today. The Bible even begins that way, "In the beginning God created the heavens and the earth." We can't ask, "I wonder what's going to happen in this story?"

Even though we know what's going to happen, we only have God's side of the conversation. God says, "Let us go down and confuse their languages . . ." Who is God talking to? It's probably the other heavenly beings, the sons (and daughters?) of God. We know there is no "Mrs. God" in the Bible, but if there were, maybe the conversation would have gone like this.

She begins, "Why are you so worried?"

"Because those people down there are building a tower and it's almost to our doorstep."

"So?"

"Think what that will do to our neighborhood. The price of real estate will plummet. We don't want nosy neighbors moving that close to us."

"It might be nice to have neighbors."

"Have you forgotten what they are like? Some of them prefer car keys to Q-Tips. One of their hobbies is taxidermy. They don't mow their grass. And when they do, they discover old cars. Do you want that in our backyard? And their kids will stomp all over the flower garden."

"They wouldn't dare. Hmmm … maybe you're right. What do you intend to do about it?"

"I was thinking of confusing them so that they cannot understand each other. Like all of a sudden making them speak different languages."

"That would be cruel."

"Yes, but it would put a stop them getting in and building on our street."

"Well, now … wait a second. Won't that create problems within families? They won't be able to understand each other."

"Teenagers already don't speak the same language as their parents."

"Yes, and the couples already communicate like the men are from Mars and the women from Venus."

"What do you mean?"

"Never mind."

"So we could make them speak different languages. Still, I don't think that would be enough to discourage them."

"Why not?"

"Because if they stay together, someone will get a copy of Rosetta Stone and they will figure out how to translate one another's languages."

"What do you propose?"

"Let's scatter them around the world. That way if they are speaking Swahili in Africa, it will be unlikely that they will get together with the people speaking Saxon in Europe. Perhaps the barriers of geography and language will be enough to prevent them from working their way up here again."

"Great plan. It will make them suspicious of each other."

"And they will fear each other because they are so different."

"What do you think about painting them different colors?"

"Why?"

"If they see people who look different, they may not even try to speak to them. It will be another way of creating suspicion and division."

"That's brilliant. What colors did you have in mind?"

"I was thinking we could use the colors in the rainbow."

"You are going too far with this. We created them in our image to look like us. I don't want people going around thinking I'm green like the giant in that vegetable commercial."

"Well, what colors would *you* prefer?"

"Let's make them subtler—just different hues—some darker, some lighter, maybe fifty shades of brown."

"But do you think that will be enough to create divisions?"

"We'll see."

26
Time to Leave the Nest

Now the Lord said to Abram, "Go from your country and your kindred and your father's house to the land that I will show you. I will make of you a great nation, and I will bless you, and make your name great, so that you will be a blessing. I will bless those who bless you, and the one who curses you I will curse; and in you all the families of the earth shall be blessed."

So Abram went, as the Lord had told him; and Lot went with him. Abram was seventy-five years old when he departed from Haran. Abram took his wife Sarai and his brother's son Lot, and all the possessions that they had gathered, and the persons whom they had acquired in Haran; and they set forth to go to the land of Canaan. When they had come to the land of Canaan, Abram passed through the land to the place at Shechem, to the oak of Moreh. At that time the Canaanites were in the land. Then the Lord appeared to Abram, and said, "To

your offspring I will give this land." So he built there an
altar to the Lord, who had appeared to him. From there
he moved on to the hill country on the east of Bethel, and
pitched his tent, with Bethel on the west and Ai on the
east; and there he built an altar to the Lord and invoked
the name of the Lord. And Abram journeyed on by stages
toward the Negeb.

Genesis 12:1-9

*G*od serves as Abram's travel agent. Of course, this is before the travel industry really takes off. But from the looks of things, business is picking up. First, God had sent Adam and Eve out of the Garden, then Cain on a world tour, the tower builders to various locations, and now Abram and Sarai on an adventure travel excursion to another country with no return ticket. Although God doesn't provide a travel brochure or a map for Abram, he promises to show Abram the sights. Then God offers an early form of travel insurance—*I will bless those who bless you and curse those who curse you.* It's not clear what kind of medical coverage comes with that.

God tells Abram to go and He probably promises he will have a good time. More than that, He promises that Abram will have children, grandchildren and many descendants on this adventure and that they will become a great nation. Apparently, God is also in the business of family planning. A sort of fertility concierge.

Abram's father Terah had apparently also wanted to go to Canaan. *Terah took his son Abram and his grandson Lot son of Haran, and his daughter-in-law Sarai, his son Abram's wife, and they went out together from Ur of the Chaldeans to go into the land of Canaan; but when they came to Haran, they settled there* (Genesis 11:31).

Perhaps Terah had seen the ads for the Mediterranean beaches or watched the land deal promos about how the land flowed with milk and honey. So, Terah set out to go there from Ur in southern Mesopotamia, but for some reason he stopped and settled in Haran in northern Mesopotamia.

In those days kids respected their elders. Sons were also servants. One day they might become Papa to their own clan and be the one in charge. Life back then was not a democracy; it was a patriarchal world. Dad made *all* the decisions. Oh, for the good old days.

Normally children did not move away from their parents. It's like the "hollers" where my father grew up in Appalachia. The parents had a home up the holler, and all the children (usually sons) had places with their spouses and kids farther down the holler. Everyone was related in the holler. Of course, if the IRS or ATF (Alcohol, Tobacco, and Firearms) comes after you, you might leave the holler to protect the secret location of the family still.

Abram and Sarai's holler is hollow at this point. They have no children. In fact, they don't have their own holler in this new land. Abram lives a semi-nomadic life with flocks of sheep and goats. Terah is 145 years old and Abram is 75 when he leaves for Canaan. If Abram had had children, Terah probably would not have let them leave. When my wife and I left the United States to serve as missionaries in Brazil, we committed the unpardonable sin by taking our parents' grandchildren overseas.

But Terah gives his blessing to his son.

"I am so glad you are going to visit the Med, son. The documentaries on beach life there make me want to come with you. By the way, if Sarai is going to fit in, she'll have to let go of her veil and most everything else."

"You never let me watch those documentaries."

"When you get your own TV, you can watch what you want. You're 75 years old and still too young to watch those PG-85 shows. By the way, I was hoping you would at least plant the crops before you leave."

"Dad, you're still spry enough to do it. You're a young 145."

"You young people are always in a hurry to leave home. It seems like yesterday that I was watching your mother change your diapers."

"Let's not get personal, Dad."

"When you get to the Mediterranean, be sure to text me a photo of ladies, I mean, locals on the beach, son."

"Like I said, Dad, you're a young 145."

The call to leave and go to Canaan includes God's promises to Abram—blessing, many descendants, and owning the land. What does Abram have to do to receive these rewards? He has to go to Canaan, which he does. Like Noah, Abram obeys God.

Later Abram will discover that God would require much more. This is shrewd on God's part. If God had told Abram about the requirement for circumcision before left he Haran, I think Abram would have said, "Lord, I'm sure Canaan is nice, but Mom & Dad are getting up in years, and they need me. Besides I'm not into traveling that much. The motels all have bed bugs, and some charge for WIFI."

Over the years, many people have learned this technique from God, which is to only reveal the full picture as the person needs to know.

Car salesman have been using it for years. After you get over the sticker shock, you learn the "out-the-door" price is much higher still.

Think of military recruiters who will list the educational advantages of serving one's country. How many people in boot camp have cursed their recruiter? It's not that they *lied*, they just did not reveal the whole truth. Okay. Maybe they lied.

It's like finding out that you will be your fiancé's third wife only as you are providing information at the courthouse for the marriage license. This is very biblical.

If I had known all that would be required of me as a pastor before I was ordained, I'd probably be a college professor in mathematics. At least then things would have added up. I'm not accusing God of "bait and switch," mind you. It's more like the complete requirements are only revealed much later in the process. Then you find out you are not on a boat gliding along to the music of "It's a Small World." Rather, you are blindfolded, seated backward, being jerked right and left, plunged straight down and snatched back up on Mr. Toad's Wild Ride.

Following God always involves adventure travel—without the insurance.

Blessed assurance, yes. Insurance, no.

27
Abram Is No Romeo

Now there was a famine in the land. So Abram went down to Egypt to reside there as an alien, for the famine was severe in the land. When he was about to enter Egypt, he said to his wife Sarai, "I know well that you are a woman beautiful in appearance; and when the Egyptians see you, they will say, 'This is his wife'; then they will kill me, but they will let you live. Say you are my sister, so that it may go well with me because of you, and that my life may be spared on your account." When Abram entered Egypt the Egyptians saw that the woman was very beautiful. When the officials of Pharaoh saw her, they praised her to Pharaoh. And the woman was taken into Pharaoh's house. And for her sake he dealt well with Abram; and he had sheep, oxen, male donkeys, male and female slaves, female donkeys, and camels.

But the Lord afflicted Pharaoh and his house with great plagues because of Sarai, Abram's wife. So Pharaoh called

Abram, and said, "What is this you have done to me? Why did you not tell me that she was your wife? Why did you say, 'She is my sister,' so that I took her for my wife? Now then, here is your wife, take her, and be gone." And Pharaoh gave his men orders concerning him; and they set him on the way, with his wife and all that he had.

Genesis 12:10-20

This is not Abram's finest hour. However, in his defense, he is practical and proactive. His drop-dead gorgeous wife, at 65 years of age, regularly wins the Mrs. Senior Palestine Beauty Contest. Pharaoh, who has a harem of young women, will not be able to resist the allure of the senior Mrs. Abram. Knowing this, Abram devises a plan.

"When we get there, honey, sweetie pie, because you are so ravishingly beautiful—as I tell you all the time—the king will surely take you from me and will kill me."

"That sounds like a problem for you," Sarai responds.

"Don't you care about me, honey? Aren't you the least little bit concerned?"

"Well, maybe the least little bit. Okay, what do you want me to do?"

Abram explains, "It's easy really. Just say you are my sister, and don't act like my wife in public."

"You mean I should not walk ten steps behind you out of deference to you, my lord?"

"No. Of course, you must walk ten steps behind me. That is where all women belong. But I'll pass you off as my sister. Then the king of Egypt will pay me a hefty bride price for you, and I'll be rich. I mean, if they think you are my wife, they will take you anyway because no one can resist your desert beauty and charm."

Sarai ruminates, "I've heard the Pharaoh is extremely wealthy. I've also heard he has a great spa. The women get manicures and pedicures. They get their hair done daily in the latest styles. I can just picture myself wearing the finest jewelry and latest fashions."

"Yes, dear, you would outshine them all. Now until we get there make sure you keep using that wrinkle cream that I gave you last year. I'm sure you will become the new queen of Egypt. Just think of all that gold and diamonds. You will sit next to the most powerful man on earth. Everyone will bow before you and give you honor."

"I guess worse things can happen than being Queen of Egypt. Of course, you will be rewarded handsomely for bringing such a fine woman as myself to rule over Egypt."

Abram says, "Pharaoh doesn't know what he's in for."

"What was that?"

"Ahem … I said, 'You'll be a blessing for sure.'"

Word of Sarai's beauty reaches Pharaoh. The king orders Abram and Sarai to be brought to him.

Pharaoh says, "So, Mr. Abram, I'm told you have a beautiful sister."

"Why, yes, your majesty, most honorable and glorious King of Egypt."

"She is of marriageable age?"

"Just barely. But the king has so many women already. Certainly, the king would have no interest in a desert beauty. Before we moved to Palestine, she won, Miss Mesopotamia 37 ... I mean, she won several years in a row."

"Step forward, young lady. Would you do me the courtesy of removing your veil?"

Sarai bows then curtsies and removes her veil. She says, "It is an honor to come before the most powerful and generous king of all the world. The women in your harem are the luckiest women alive. To be in your presence must make them thank the gods every day. I am your servant. Do with me as you wish."

"Didn't I see you in an Oil of Olay commercial twenty-five years ago?"

"No, my lord, I've only modeled for Revlon."

"Mr. Abram, how high is the bride price? How much are you asking for her?"

Abram negotiates. "Well, I had not intended to marry off my sister at her tender age. However, you are the king of Egypt. How could I ask for a better brother-in-law? I don't ask for much, just enough to make me extremely wealthy by Egyptian standards. One of your Rolls would be nice, and that red Ferrari with your best mechanic. And how about your beach house on the Mediterranean, with the housekeepers thrown in?"

Pharaoh barters. "Will you settle for sheep, oxen, male donkeys, male and female slaves, female donkeys, and camels and enough gold and silver to fill a bushel basket each?"

Abram caves. "You drive a hard bargain. I accept."

Sarai says, "Dear *brother*, may I have a moment with you in private?" Pulling him aside, she says, "Is that all you think I'm worth? I can't believe you are going to sell me for such a trifle. I'm worth ten times that. What's wrong with you?"

Abram turns back to the Pharaoh. "A thousand apologies for the interruption, your highness. Even someone as great as you, Pharaoh, cannot resist her charms. *Please* take her. Take her now."

28
Origin of the Baptists

*Now Abram was very rich in livestock, in silver, and
in gold. He journeyed on by stages from the Negeb as
far as Bethel, to the place where his tent had been at the
beginning, between Bethel and Ai, to the place where he
had made an altar at the first; and there Abram called on
the name of the Lord. Now Lot, who went with Abram,
also had flocks and herds and tents, so that the land
could not support both of them living together; for their
possessions were so great that they could not live together,
and there was strife between the herders of Abram's
livestock and the herders of Lot's livestock. At that time the
Canaanites and the Perizzites lived in the land.*

*Then Abram said to Lot, "Let there be no strife between
you and me, and between your herders and my herders; for
we are kindred. Is not the whole land before you? Separate
yourself from me. If you take the left hand, then I will go
to the right; or if you take the right hand, then I will go to*

the left." Lot looked about him and saw that the plain of
the Jordan was well watered everywhere like the garden
of the Lord, like the land of Egypt, in the direction of
Zoar; this was before the Lord had destroyed Sodom and
Gomorrah. So Lot chose for himself all the plain of the
Jordan, and Lot journeyed eastward; thus they separated
from each other. Abram settled in the land of Canaan,
while Lot settled among the cities of the Plain and moved
his tent as far as Sodom.

Genesis 13:2-12

*W*hy is Abram so rich? Oh, that's right …
he swindled the bride price for Sarai from
Pharaoh. That one act made him extremely wealthy,
which in those days was measured by livestock. But
Abram and his nephew Lot had so many flocks and
herds it created a problem—their herders competed
over land to graze their animals.

Can't you hear cowboy Abram say in his best
Mesopotamian drawl, "This land ain't big enough for
you and me both, Boy. Pick yer land." The story gives
the impression that Abram is in charge of all of it.
While it was true that God had promised him the land,
in reality it belonged to the Canaanites and Perizzites.

Uncle Abram is very gracious and allows Lot to
have his choice of where to graze his animals. Lot
chooses the well-watered land along the Jordan River.

Lot picks the Jordan plain, but ends up down south by the Dead Sea in Sodom, which, by the way, does not end so well. Abram is left with the less-desirable hill country and the arid south.

(I used to be Baptist. It was a long time ago. Most Protestant denominations trace their beginnings to sometime after Martin Luther posted his 95 Theses on the Wittenberg Church door 500 years ago. However, some Baptists point back 2,000 years to John the Baptist as their founder. While studying at a Baptist seminary, I learned that Baptists actually go back much further in history—four thousand years, in fact—all the way back to Abram & Lot. The Baptist movement began when Abram said to Lot, "You go your way and I'll go mine.")

Sometimes the best solution is to put distance between family members. When my brother and I could not get along, Mom separated us. I guess she got the idea early in her marriage because she always said she loved her mother-in-law, but it was easier to love her from a distance. She considered 1,000 miles or more a right-fine distance.

So, the Baptists figured this out long ago. That's why there are more than 60 national bodies of Baptist churches in the United States alone. When you can't get along with other people in your church, what do you do? Break off and start your own church. This is the Baptist way of church growth. Division leads to multiplication. In my home town there are at least three Baptist churches that all came from the same church.

Of course, they don't talk to each other …

Separations can lead to peace. Abram and Lot part amicably.

Abram says to Lot, "I'll miss playing checkers with you by the campfire, nephew."

To which Lot responds, "Who's going to wash your Mercedes when I'm gone, Uncle Abram?"

"We'll manage. I will miss our long talks about what fun we had in Egypt when your aunt was . . . Oops, here she comes."

Sarai joins in, "Don't think I didn't hear you. I had fun at the Pharaoh's palace, too."

"What kind of fun?" asks Abram.

"Wouldn't you like to know," Sarai teases.

"You didn't . . . He didn't . . ." stammers Abram.

Sarai responds, "I was treated like a queen. But it didn't last long. At least the Pharaoh did the right thing. All because you were a coward."

"Now, honey, let's not be calling names."

"You're the one giving the labels. Calling me your sister instead of your wife so you could make a bundle of money from selling me."

Abram pleads, "What else was I supposed to do? They would have taken you from me and have killed me. Everyone knows you're the most beautiful woman in the world—even at 65."

Sarai snaps, "What was that? Did you say something about my age? There you go with the age thing again."

"But it all worked out. Thank God."

"That's one thing we agree on."

Lot chimes in, "I'm going to miss both of you—even your quarreling. It's kind of cute."

29
The Gift of Procrastination

The Lord said to Abram, after Lot had separated from him, "Raise your eyes now, and look from the place where you are, northward and southward and eastward and westward; for all the land that you see I will give to you and to your offspring forever. I will make your offspring like the dust of the earth; so that if one can count the dust of the earth, your offspring also can be counted. Rise up, walk through the length and the breadth of the land, for I will give it to you." So Abram moved his tent, and came and settled by the oaks of Mamre, which are at Hebron; and there he built an altar to the Lord.

Genesis 13:14-18

Imagine you have a billionaire uncle who promises to leave you his entire estate in his will. He invites you to visit the property, to sleep in the 147 different bedrooms, and to explore the thousands of acres of lakes, rolling hills and forests. Wouldn't that be exciting? It would be even more exciting if your uncle was 97 years old with a bad cough.

God promises the land to Abram in the passage above and in Genesis 12:7, 15:18-19, and 17:8. God tells him to travel through the land, check it out, because he and his family will own it. But God does not get bad coughs. God is eternal. And there is no date on the promise to Abram.

Abram never owns the land, never controls the land. Others, who were more powerful than Abram, control cities and territories in Canaan. When Sarah dies, Abram has to buy a little plot of land from a Hittite to bury her. Neither his son Isaac, nor his grandson Jacob, nor his twelve great-grandsons own the land. They are only a tiny minority among the stronger peoples of Palestine who possess the real estate.

Abram's descendants do not own the entire land of Palestine until David reigns somewhere around 1000 BCE—800 years or more after God made this promise.

Notice the future tense here: *for the all land that you see I will give to you*. Abram does not own it then, but one day he will. This was genius on God's part. God tells Abram this so many times, it becomes part of the family folklore.

This is a shrewd gift strategy on God's part. You promise a great gift, but keep putting off delivering the gift. I've promised my wife that one of these days we will go to Hawaii for our wedding anniversary. "We can't afford it this year, honey, but maybe next year." Hawaiian hope springs eternal.

Of course, one day a good man must keep his promise. This is where God has a huge advantage over us. Being eternal is a major perk of divinity. You can make a promise to a man like Abram and his descendants; so what if it takes 800 years for you to keep it?

Is this one of those "rent-to-own" deals on God's part? "Abram, I'll rent you the land. All I ask in return is that you make sacrifices and remain loyal to me. Then *one day* I'll give you and your descendants the land."

It's a great deal for God. They make sacrifices to God and are loyal to God, at least part of the time, for 800 years before they possess all the land.

Abram is long dead before God fulfills the promise. Does this create a problem for God? Is Abraham up in heaven asking every few weeks for 800 years, "So when are you going to give the land to my people?" Sort of like kids in the backseat asking every five minutes during a ten-hour trip, "Are we there yet?"

Now God is gifted when it comes to procrastinating in fulfilling a promise. God gives us a great example of using the loophole of time. Never put a date on a promise. Think how that can take the stress out of relationships.

"Sure, honey, I'll marry you—one day."

"I promise if you'll keep up this great work, one day you'll get a promotion."

"Hey, kids, if you do your chores, someday I'll take you to Disney World."

There is no pressure to fulfill any of these because of the loophole of time and the gift of procrastination. It also gives the people who are being promised something to hope for.

As a pastor, I've had people insist that I promise to preach their funeral, especially as I was preparing to leave that area to move to another parish. At least with *that* promise I get to wait a while. Plus, I can reason that they will never see me again. If they make it to heaven, they'll forgive me, surely.

So let's take a lesson from God and learn to procrastinate—if not now, later.

30
Armed Man of Faith

Then one who had escaped came and told Abram the
Hebrew, who was living by the oaks of Mamre the
Amorite, brother of Eshcol and of Aner; these were allies
of Abram. When Abram heard that his nephew had
been taken captive, he led forth his trained men, born
in his house, three hundred eighteen of them, and went
in pursuit as far as Dan. He divided his forces against
them by night, he and his servants, and routed them
and pursued them to Hobah, north of Damascus. Then
he brought back all the goods, and also brought back his
nephew Lot with his goods, and the women and the
people.

Genesis 14:13-16

Abram says to Lot, "This is the last time I'm bailing you out of jail."

Lot responds, "But, Uncle Abram, it wasn't my fault."

"It never is. You thought that your gang could take on the others. You lost. Well I showed you whose gang is the strongest. They don't call us Abram's Rams for nothing."

"Uncle, I never even knew you had a gang. You've got more than three hundred men!"

"You thought you could beat the others, didn't you, Lot?"

"No, they attacked us. They kidnapped us."

"That's what you get for hanging out with the wrong crowd."

"We were just minding our own business. They showed up at our clubhouse."

"Didn't you remember the judo moves I showed you?"

"Yeah, but they outnumbered us. And they had spears and swords."

"I told you not to join up with that gang. What kind of name is Sodomites anyway? Sounds like you would always be taking up the rear. Haven't I always told you that fighting gets you nowhere?"

"You are right, Uncle Abram. I've learned my lesson."

"Use your head, not your fists. Remember how I stole all that money and livestock from Pharaoh? I didn't have to raise a finger to take it from him, just had to sell off Sarai as my sister."

"Right. Aunt Sarai still talks about the palace."

"Never mind her. Pharaoh gave her back to me and I didn't give the bride money back to him. That was an amazing deal. You see that's an example of how to get what you want from people."

"But I was not trying to take anything from anybody."

"Lot, that's not what the police report says."

"Really, we were just minding our own business."

"I know. I know. But aren't you glad your Uncle Abram has a gang of his own?"

"Yes, sir. Thanks, Uncle Abram, for bailing me out. It won't happen again."

"It had better not, nephew."

Abram is known as a man of faith. Imagine if every man of faith had his own 300-man army. As a pastor, it could have its advantages. Instead of parishioners giving only 1-2% of their income to the church, having a small army could help raise the level of giving. Armed ushers passing the collection plates would probably see an increase in funding.

If people "stiff" the pastor after a wedding or funeral, sending a platoon by their house as a reminder might be helpful.

Increasing more regular church attendance would be easy.

"Pastor, I told your men when they came by that I really did have the flu last Sunday. I gave them my physician's note."

"Pastor, we were in Topeka visiting family last Sunday. This clip from their surveillance video proves we were worshiping at our denominational sister church."

It would make pastoral cold calls more successful. The pastor pulls up at a prospect's home with three armed men in black suits in his Mercedes. After they exit the car, all four go up to the front door. In the meantime, the eight men in combat fatigues exit their Humvees with weapons drawn and circle the home's perimeter to prevent escape. At the door the friendly pastor grabs the homeowner's shaking hand and invites himself into the man's home followed by his security detail.

"I've heard you are looking for a church home."

"No, not really. We don't go . . ."

The two of the men closest to the homeowner reach into their suit pockets and pull out Glock pistols.

The homeowner quickly says, "I mean, yes, we were thinking about visiting . . ."

The pastor continues, "We'd love to have you check out our church. Here is a brochure with the service times."

The man is visibly trembling as he takes the brochure.

The pastor continues, "Do you have any children?

"A daughter and two sons. Why?"

"That's wonderful. What grades are they in?"

"The boys are in fourth and sixth. Our daughter is a sophomore."

"Your fourth-grader will love our Christian version of SWAT 4 video game. Your sixth-grader gets to join our exciting confirmation class this year. In addition to confirming their faith in God, they confirm their commitment to protect the clergy. He will enjoy the Rambo Confirmation Retreat. This year we will be holding the Rambo Confirmation Retreat between police training sessions on the grounds of the Police Academy. The kids are all worked up about it."

"What about my daughter? She doesn't have to . . ."

"You will be pleased to know that we are a progressive church, your daughter will be welcomed in our high school weapons training program. She will have the opportunity to qualify as an expert marksman, something more conservative churches would deny her. She'll be a real asset to law enforcement one day."

The homeowner gulps, and questions, "But, she wants to be a ballerina."

The pastor responds, "A ballerina who can take out a bad guy at 600 yards. Wouldn't that be awesome? I don't want to brag but when our young people graduate from our training course, they make fine Christian *soldiers*. All branches of the local military recruiters and law enforcement agencies have my number on speed dial."

Motioning to his security detail, the pastor says, "These gentlemen all went through our militia training before joining the Marines. They've got a ton of medals among them for outstanding service to our country. Now they are on PCP, Protecting Clergy Police. Isn't that right, gentlemen?"

They shout in unison, "Sir, yes, sir."

The new family is in church the next Sunday, and from then on.

Foreign missionaries might have an easier time of things. It would cut down on the martyrdom of missionaries if they had their own military force to defend them. Having your own militia might make it easier to communicate in any language. Most people speak AK-47.

Think of the advantage for the local ministerial associations. Combining our small armies might make it easier to combat negative influences in the community. We could more easily convert the *exotic* dancers club into a worship center for *liturgical* dance. Ringing the bell by the red kettle would bring in more donations for the poor if each passerby had a pistol waved at him or her.

But then if pastors did not want to work together, it could lead to other problems. It might make the softball game between the Baptists and Methodists a little more intense.

Abram, the father of our faith, left us a great example, not only of an entrepreneur but also of a military leader. Just think what we could do if the clergy of the three Abrahamic faiths—Judaism, Christianity, and Islam—organized their own armies.

What? Did you say something about the Crusades?

31
The Country Preach-ers' Favorite Text

After his return from the defeat of Chedorlaomer and the
kings who were with him, the king of Sodom went out
to meet him at the Valley of Shaveh (that is, the King's
Valley). And King Melchizedek of Salem brought out
bread and wine; he was priest of God Most High. He
blessed him and said,

"Blessed be Abram by God Most High,
maker of heaven and earth;
and blessed be God Most High,
who has delivered your enemies into your hand!"
And Abram gave him one-tenth of everything.

Genesis 14:17-20

*T*he country preacher steps into the pulpit,
reads the above text, then starts preaching:

"Brethren and sistern: I'll have you to know that the message of God for you today is as clear as the nose on my face, even as clear as the nose on Sister Edna's face, and that's mighty obvious. Today's message is: Abram gave a tenth and so should you! He gave a tenth to the priest. Therefore, you should give a tenth to me, which is to say, to the Lord in the collection plate. Abram gave ten percent of all that he had when he got the blessing of God. You want the blessing of God, don't you? Then put your money in. That's how it works. Thar ain't nothin' free in this world. You want to be blessed by God, you got to pay up front.

"Melchizedek brought out bread and wine, and Abram paid up. There ain't no such thing as a free lunch—not even the Lord's supper. Who do you think buys the bread and grape juice? My wife does. It costs something. It cost Jesus everything. Abram wasn't a freeloader. God don't like freeloaders—livin' off the good that others do. Abram paid up, and you, too, better pay up if you want to be blessed. God don't want no deadbeat dads or moms or grandmas or grandpas. God don't want no deadbeat Christians. You better pay up if you want to get in good with God Most High.

"My wife needs a new dress.

"Can I get an 'Amen'?"

"AMEN!"

"Thanks, honey. What a spiritual woman my wife is!

"Now, Melchizedek was priest of God Most High. We're Baptists. We ain't Catholics. We don't have priests. God sent us preachers out, of which I am the one in charge of this here church. If you don't want to offend God Most High, you don't want to offend his preacher. You don't want me to be late on the loan payment for my new F150, do you?

"Can I get a witness? Can I get a 'Praise the Lord'?"

"PRAISE THE LORD!"

"That's my daughter, full of the Spirit. She likes ridin' in the back of my new pickup, don't you, honey?

"Continuing on: God put me here to show you the way and that way is clear. Pay up. Give ten percent just like ole honest Abe did. He knew he owed God for lettin' him win the battle. So he gave ten percent of all his winnin'. Jesus said, 'Go and do likewise.'

"Now, ushers, march on down here with them collection plates. Make sure everyone pays. We don't want no one to offend God Most High this mornin'. His wrath is somethin' to behold. You know what he did to Sodom and Gomorrah. You don't want fire and brimstone rainin' down on your house, do you? Speakin' of which, my house payment is due this week. So, you better pay up now.

"Can I get a 'Glory?'"

"GLORY!"

"Thanks, son. Isn't he a great church treasurer? And he's just a teenager. No doubt, he'll be a preacher, too, one day.

"Remember: ten percent—that's the minimum for keepin' in God's good graces.

"Don't look back after you give your ten percent in regret. Remember Lot's wife. She looked back at what she had and God turned her into a salt mannequin. She's still out there near the Dead Sea—a pillar of salt. For what? For regrettin' what she gave up. Don't you be regrettin' what you give. She left ever'thing because the angels told her to. God ain't askin' for much—just ten percent, just your tithe. Jesus paid it all. And what does He ask of you? Why ten percent ain't even a good tip. You should put in more. God loves a cheerful giver. Be like Father Abram and be blessed.

"Can I get a 'Hallelujah?'"

"HALLELUJAH!"

32
God Walks the Gauntlet

*After these things the word of the Lord came to Abram
in a vision, "Do not be afraid, Abram, I am your
shield; your reward shall be very great." But Abram
said, "O Lord God, what will you give me, for I
continue childless, and the heir of my house is Eliezer of
Damascus?" And Abram said, "You have given me no
offspring, and so a slave born in my house is to be my
heir." But the word of the Lord came to him, "This man
shall not be your heir; no one but your very own issue
shall be your heir." He brought him outside and said,
"Look toward heaven and count the stars, if you are
able to count them." Then he said to him, "So shall your*

descendants be." And he believed the Lord; and the Lord reckoned it to him as righteousness.

Genesis 15:1-6

*I*t's hard for us to imagine just how frustrating not having an heir in the ancient world was. There is no evidence that Abram believes in or understands the concept of life after death. A man lives beyond his own death through the descendants and in the memory of his family, and Abram has no child. But God keeps promising him descendants. In this chapter, God promises again that he *will* have a son. God shows him the stars and tells him to count them. We don't know how far Abram has gotten in school, but we assume he can count into the thousands. God's point is clear. Abram will have a son and from that son, he will have many descendants. Abram's response is to believe God. But the very next paragraph has Abram doubting the promise about the land.

Then he said to him, "I am the Lord who brought you from Ur of the Chaldeans, to give you this land to possess." But he said, "O Lord God, how am I to know that I shall possess it?" (Genesis 15:7-8).

Believing he will father a child is apparently easier than believing he will possess the land of Palestine. So God takes a different approach. We might say God runs the gauntlet.

He said to him, "Bring me a heifer three years old, a female goat three years old, a ram three years old, a turtledove, and a young pigeon." He brought him all these and cut them in two, laying each half over against the other; but he did not cut the birds in two. And when birds of prey came down on the carcasses, Abram drove them away. As the sun was going down, a deep sleep fell upon Abram, and a deep and terrifying darkness descended upon him (Genesis 15:9-12).

God gives Abram a job. Abram is to take a heifer, a female goat, and a ram, each a three-year-old. He is to cut them in half, laying the halves opposite each other. Then apparently he kills a turtle dove and a pigeon. It would appear that these are some kind of sacrifice. But there is more to it than that. This is an ancient covenant ceremony.

One or both parties who are making the covenant walk between the halves of animals saying in effect, may this be done to me if I do not fulfill my part of the covenant. This ancient ceremony explains the expression in Hebrew "to cut a covenant," which is usually translated into English "to make a covenant."

The amazing thing about this covenant is what Abram sees in his dream. *When the sun had gone down and it was dark, a smoking fire pot and a flaming torch passed between these pieces. On that day the Lord made a covenant with Abram, saying, "To your descendants I give this land, from the river of Egypt to the great river, the river Euphrates . . ."* (Genesis 15:17-18)

The smoke and the fire represent God's presence. Is God saying, "May I end up like these animals if I do not give you this land"? It is a bizarre but remarkable scene.

Think about what would happen if we adopted this form of making covenants. What would it do to the marriage ceremony? For sure, it would change decorating for a wedding. Imagine the bride walking down the aisle with halves of animals on either side. In fact, this concept would change the whole wedding *industry* ... and lead to many more outdoor weddings. It also might make it harder to recruit bridesmaids. They would probably forego the six-inch stilettos in favor of galoshes.

The groom comes down the aisle and the soon-to-be mother-in-law wipes the blood off the meat cleaver as a subtle reminder. Instead of a unity candle there is the meat cleaver standing erect with its tip buried in a wooden cutting board.

The message is clear: if you don't keep your marriage vows, then you are going to end up like these animals.

(Just wondering: if you have a PETA-approved wedding, would you make papier-mâché animals and cut them in half?)

Imagine buying a house. You are going to promise to pay monthly. As you approach the sidewalk to the title agent's office for the closing, she is standing outside the door. On either side of the sidewalk are mirror-image carcass halves. She says sweetly, "Are you ready to make your commitment today?" Her assistant is standing beside her with his meat cleaver and a butcher's apron covered with blood. All this is part of your contract ... you know, so you know what you're getting into. It makes the threat of foreclosure seem tame by comparison and, call me crazy, but signing that 800-page mortgage contract suddenly seems kinda all right.

Think about a star high school football quarterback. Imagine he's going to sign a letter of intent to play football next year for Florida State University. The university would gather all the high school players who are going to commit to FSU before the homecoming game. Before the game real Seminoles would lead live alligators on leashes around the field in a display of what is to come.

At half-time they would cart the gator carcass halves onto the field and lay them opposite each other from one goal line to the other. Then the incoming quarterback would lead the freshman class in a slow walk through the gator halves while the cheerleaders lead the crowd in war whoops accompanied by the tomahawk chop. The band would probably not take to the field again. The second half might have a bit sloppier playing surface.

I imagine a couple new industries would develop—covenant insurance and covenant security. This would be in case you had to default on your promise. Covenant insurance would provide a band of attorneys to take legal action on your behalf. Covenant security would also provide 24/7 bodyguards to protect you against the possibility of being kidnapped and halved.

33
Whatever You Want, Sweetie

Now Sarai, Abram's wife, bore him no children. She had an Egyptian slave-girl whose name was Hagar, and Sarai said to Abram, "You see that the Lord has prevented me from bearing children; go in to my slave-girl; it may be that I shall obtain children by her." And Abram listened to the voice of Sarai. So, after Abram had lived ten years in the land of Canaan, Sarai, Abram's wife, took Hagar the Egyptian, her slave-girl, and gave her to her husband Abram as a wife. He went in to Hagar, and she conceived; and when she saw that she had conceived, she looked with contempt on her mistress. Then Sarai said to Abram, "May the wrong done to me be on you! I gave my slave-girl to your embrace, and when she saw that she had conceived, she looked on me with contempt. May the Lord judge between you and me!" But Abram said to Sarai, "Your

slave-girl is in your power; do to her as you please." Then
Sarai dealt harshly with her, and she ran away from her.

Genesis 16:1-6

*T*his story contains a miracle—a husband listens to his wife. Seriously. How often does *that* happen? But then, how often does a wife say, "Honey, I want you to sleep with my maid"?

Sarai attempts to convince Abram. "Sweetie, I know I'm asking a lot, but I think you should sleep with Hagar. She's pretty and young and . . ." By this time, Abram has already escorted Hagar into the bedroom, drawn the curtains, locked the door, and hung the "Do Not Disturb" sign on the doorknob.

Some preachers and writers of Sunday school literature condemn Abram and Sarai for doing this. They accuse them of lack of faith and immorality. However, they are wrong on both counts. First, Sarai had tremendous faith. She really believed her eighty-five-year-old husband could impregnate her maid (and this was long before Viagra). Second, evidence from the Ancient Near East confirms that this was a common practice. In fact, after being married for ten years and not producing a child for her husband, a woman was legally obligated in some Ancient Near East cultures to provide a surrogate. However, the child born to the surrogate would be considered the (first) wife's.

In contrast to our world today, children were considered assets in the ancient world. First, they were free labor; you didn't have to pay them. You only had to feed them if they produced something to eat. And if you had enough offspring, retirement came early.

My folks would have made excellent ancient-world parents. They were apparently unaware of modern child labor laws. We were always expected to work. At one point, we planted a huge garden—about the size of all the parking lots at Disney World combined. Planting seeds, weeding, cultivating, and harvesting were all done by hand. We worked on our hands and knees or bent over in the heat of the summer. Then we had to assist in the canning process, which went on until spring planting rolled around again.

When I had to report on my summer vacation at school in the fall, I showed them the blisters on my hands and the dirt under my fingernails and wept openly. For Show and Tell, I brought in three bushels of tomatoes, seventy-five cucumbers, four dozen ears of corn, seventeen cantaloupes, and eight watermelons. When I tried to sell them to the other kids at recess, the teacher said that was against school rules and confiscated everything.

Sarai's faith in her husband is rewarded. Hagar becomes pregnant, but things go downhill from there. Sarai feels shame for not having done her wifely duty—

which was to produce children. But Hagar makes it worse by rubbing Sarai's nose in it.

Hagar says, "Obviously God, like, approves of my being Abram's wife, and not you. Old woman, he's my husband now. You have been replaced, you poor wrinkled thing. Obviously, I know how to please a man, which is more than I can say for you. From now on you can wash my clothes, do the cooking and do the dishes. I am like his number-one wife now. I did for him what you could not do. He loves my smooth young skin. Your Oil of Olay quit working decades ago, honey. He wants to enter me in the Mrs. Palestine Beauty Contest. He said you won. But then he laughed and said it was so long ago, all the judges are long dead. Their grandkids are now the judges and they're older than I am. What was the beauty contest last century? I bet your swimsuits were, like, those ancient onesies that went down to your knees."

I can see it now. After the first night Hagar moves all Sarai's things from the bedroom out to the guest tent. She takes a photo of Sarai carrying the laundry in one hand using her cane with the other. Hagar sends Sarai's photo to her friends on VeilBook, then breaks out laughing at the responses. Hagar later tells Abram that Sarai's photo has gone viral. Sarai doesn't believe it because she is feeling fine and does not even have a sniffle. It does not help that Abram laughs at everything that little snot says, especially when she makes fun of the old woman. He walks everywhere with a spring in his step and a smile on his face.

That is too much for Sarai. She takes aim at Hagar. "You and your friends are making fun of me for using this cane. Let's see if you like how it feels." With that she raises her walking stick and hobbles toward Hagar. But Hagar is too quick and sidesteps Sarai's intended blow. Sarai stumbles and falls.

This infuriates Sarai. She calls for Abram to help her get up off the ground. As soon as she is on her feet, she turns on Abram. She reminds him she is still his number-one wife. She still wears the panties in the family. She unleashes an old-world curse on him, bringing the threat of the wrath of God down on him. Hagar has been elevated to the status of second wife by Sarai's offer and by Abram's sleeping with her.

Some would call Abram a coward. However, I think Abram demonstrates wisdom. He realizes that he is not going to be able to mediate a conflict between two wives under the same canvas. Sarai and Hagar are two of the most strong-willed women described in the Bible. If Abram steps between that lion and that tiger clawing at each other, he is going to be the loser. So he, in effect, demotes Hagar back to slave-girl status, giving Sarai permission to do what she wants to her (not his finest moment).

Abram has learned the secret to being married so long—how to say "yes, dear" with a straight face. Here he uses the variation, "Do whatever you want, honey. You're in charge."

It could very well be that Abram is the author of that ancient proverb: A man who says he's boss at home will lie about other things, too.

34
Wild Ass of a Man?
Not a Doctor or a
Lawyer?

The angel of the Lord found her by a spring of water in the wilderness, the spring on the way to Shur. And he said, "Hagar, slave-girl of Sarai, where have you come from and where are you going?" She said, "I am running away from my mistress Sarai." The angel of the Lord said to her, "Return to your mistress, and submit to her." The angel of the Lord also said to her, "I will so greatly multiply your offspring that they cannot be counted for multitude." And the angel of the Lord said to her,

"Now you have conceived and shall bear a son;
you shall call him Ishmael,
for the Lord has given heed to your affliction.
He shall be a wild ass of a man,
with his hand against everyone,

and everyone's hand against him;
and he shall live at odds with all his kin."

So she named the Lord who spoke to her, "You are El-roi;"
for she said, "Have I really seen God and remained alive
after seeing him?" Therefore the well was called Beer-
lahai-roi; it lies between Kadesh and Bered.

Genesis 16:7-14

One day God gave out assignments to the angels in heaven. It's Angel Roy's first day on the job and God says to him, "I want you to go down to earth and tell the Egyptian slave-girl Hagar to go back to her mistress, back to Sarai."

Angel Roy says, "You know my family is from Egypt, don't you?"

"She needs to go back."

"Let me get this straight. You want me to send a runaway slave girl back to the one who is abusing her? And I thought you were supposed to be fair."

"I'm concerned about her. She won't survive in the wilderness."

"But are you sure she'll survive Sarai's abuse?"

"You have to convince her to go back."

"How can I do that?"

"Let her know I've heard her cries for help, that she is going to have a son, and that she should name him Ishmael."

"What if she's picked out other boy names, like Fred or John or Abe, Jr.?"

"In Hebrew Ishmael means 'God heard.' Tell her to call him Ishmael, because I have heard her cries for help."

"Don't you think Abram should get to vote on his firstborn's name?"

"Tell her I promise that she will be the mother of many descendants."

"And that's supposed to win her over? Sounds like a lot of mouths to feed to me."

"Let her know that her son will be *a wild ass of a man*."

"Seriously? What kind of career track is that? Don't you think she would rather have her son be a doctor or attorney? How's he going to support her in her old age?"

"Inform her that her son will be a wild ass of a man who will pick fights with everyone, even all his relatives."

"God, I think you are out of touch with earthlings. I'm not sure that's what every mother dreams for her son to grow up to be. Moms want their sons to be successful with a lot of money, land, and security. That way they can take care of their mothers when they grow old."

"Angel Roy, you are new at this. But I have confidence you will deliver my message. Besides, if you don't do as I say, there is another place you can live. It's quite warm this time of year. In fact, all times of the year." Then God laughs so hard it thunders.

Angel Roy goes down and finds Hagar at a spring. "What's happening, Hagar?" he asks.

"Who are you?"

"I've come from God with a message."

"Yeah, right. And I'm the Queen of Sheba."

"Seriously. God sent me because God is concerned about you."

"*Nobody* cares about me."

"God cares about everybody."

"Let's say I believe you. What's the message?"

"Well, I've got good news and bad news. Which do you want?"

"Is this some kind of stupid joke?"

"No."

"Give me the bad news. It can't get any worse."

"You have to go back to Sarai."

"I was wrong. It can get worse. Are you crazy? She'll kill me. She beat me so bad I was afraid I'd lose my baby."

"That's the good news. You are going to have a baby boy."

"Really? I know Abram wanted a boy. That will make him so happy. That is good news."

"God says you are supposed to name the boy *Ishmael*."

"Why Ishmael? What if we had already picked out Fred, John or Abe, Jr.?"

"Ishmael means 'God heard.' Hagar, you should know that God has heard your cries for help."

"If that's true, why would he send me back there?"

"It's for your own good. You can't survive out here in the wilderness. It's no place for a woman in your condition."

"Since you know so much, what is Ishmael going to be like? What is he going to grow up to be?"

"He's going to grow up to be a lot like you. He'll be independent, strong, not afraid of conflict, a fighter, ready to take on anyone."

"Are you referring to my making fun of Sarai and kicking her out of Abram's bedroom? She deserved it, that old hag. If I wasn't afraid of Abram, I'd knock her into the next country."

"There is more good news. Ishmael will be free. He won't be a slave to anyone."

"Then he can take care of me. What kind of career will he have?"

"Well ... I'm—uh ... I'm not sure of the specifics."

"Tell me! Don't hold back or I'll ruffle those wings of yours."

Angel Roy jumps back. "Let's not get violent. God said Ishmael will be *a wild ass of a man.*"

Hagar smiles. "I love it. Free to be himself out in the world on his own terms, not taken advantage of and abused like his mom."

"You're happy about that?"

"You bet. Now I know God has heard me. I will have a son, and he will be free. Not only that, God sees me. You saw me here and came to rescue me. I'm calling you, "El-Roi," which means 'God sees me.'"

And that's *really* how Angel Roy got his name.

35
You Want Me to Cut Off What?

*When Abram was ninety-nine years old, the Lord
appeared to Abram, and said to him, "I am God Almighty;
walk before me, and be blameless. And I will make
my covenant between me and you, and will make you
exceedingly numerous." Then Abram fell on his face; and
God said to him, "As for me, this is my covenant with you:
You shall be the ancestor of a multitude of nations. No
longer shall your name be Abram, but your name shall be
Abraham; for I have made you the ancestor of a multitude
of nations. I will make you exceedingly fruitful; and I
will make nations of you, and kings shall come from you.
I will establish my covenant between me and you, and
your offspring after you throughout their generations, for
an everlasting covenant, to be God to you and to your
offspring after you. And I will give to you, and to your*

offspring after you, the land where you are now an alien,
all the land of Canaan, for a perpetual holding; and I will
be their God."

God said to Abraham, "As for you, you shall keep my
covenant, you and your offspring after you throughout
their generations. This is my covenant, which you shall
keep, between me and you and your offspring after you:
Every male among you shall be circumcised. You shall
circumcise the flesh of your foreskins, and it shall be a sign
of the covenant between me and you. Throughout your
generations every male among you shall be circumcised
when he is eight days old, including the slave born in
your house and the one bought with your money from any
foreigner who is not of your offspring. Both the slave born
in your house and the one bought with your money must
be circumcised. So shall my covenant be in your flesh an
everlasting covenant. Any uncircumcised male who is not
circumcised in the flesh of his foreskin shall be cut off from
his people; he has broken my covenant."

Genesis 17:1-9

*T*he Lord appears to the ninety-nine-year-old Abram and says, "Abram, I am making a covenant with you."

"Yes, Lord, we've talked about this before. You promised me a son and many descendants, and they will possess the land. I am very honored and grateful."

"Yes, but we have not talked about what I expect of *you*, Abram."

"What do you mean? You asked me to leave my family and move to Canaan, which I did. That was an expensive move, by the way. Sarai is still going on about how the movers damaged some of our furniture."

"I want you to follow my rules."

"What rules? We never talked about rules before."

"Every covenant has rules."

"Okay, fine, but I want to see the details in writing."

"Suit yourself."

God hands Abram a copy of the contract.

"Let me look at this deal. This is not my name. My name is Abram, not Abraham. And it's Sarai, not Sarah. This must be for another couple."

God says under his breath, "Drat! It's so hard to get a good scribe."

Then God says to Abraham, "I'm changing your names as part of this new written contract. Don't you like Abraham better than Abram? Abraham means 'father of multitudes.' It gives you hope for many grandchildren."

The newly-appointed Abraham, Father of Multitudes, nods his approval. "It does have a nice ring to it."

God explains, "*Sarah* is just another form of *Sarai*. Both names mean "princess."

"I thought *Sarai* meant "contentious." That fits her better. Princess? She would love that. I wouldn't be surprised if that's what Pharaoh called her."

"Let's not bring that fiasco up again. I saved you from that disaster. Again, what were you thinking?"

Abraham's eyes continue to roam over the contract until—"Wait! It says here I'm supposed to be blameless? Nobody's perfect, you know. Well, except for you, Lord. Aren't you setting the bar too high?"

"Haven't you heard of Noah? He was blameless."

"Yeah, but I'm not that good with animals. And what's *this* fine print? It's hard to read. This big word here—Cir-cum-ci-sion? I don't know what that means. I'm not an attorney."

"A minor surgery I expect of you and all the men and boys among your people."

"What kind of surgery?"

"Just a little snip here and another snip there." God leans over and whispers in Abraham's ear.

Abraham responds in disbelief, "You want me to cut off *what*? You call *that* minor? No way! Are you crazy? Look, we had a deal. All I had to do was to come to this place and you would bless me."

"And I have blessed you".

"Yes, and I'm grateful. Now you expect me to be perfect, and you want me to cut off . . . What if the knife slips? Then what?"

"You have to be careful."

"What if I just cut my hair instead, or shave my beard, or trim my toenails?"

"At ninety-nine you are certainly overdue for a mani-pedi. But circumcision is what I expect of all the males."

"Nope. No way. Not going to do it."

"You'll thank me later."

"What do you mean?"

"How long has it been since you 'got lucky' with Sarah?"

"Can't remember the last time."

"Not only will you get lucky, but you'll make her pregnant."

"Right. No way. Sarai, I mean, Sarah's going to be ninety years old next year and Ishmael is well into his teens. So, pregnant? You're kidding."

"I'm serious. You will have another son."

"At my age? Really?"

"If you circumcise yourself, it will be like Viagra for you."

"What's Viagra?"

"Let's just say, you'll both thank me later."